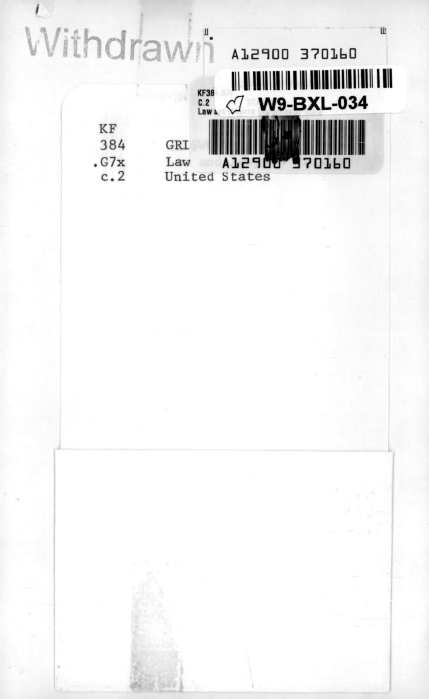

THE UNITED STATES

LAW AND LAWYERS
IN THE UNITED STATES
The Common Law Under Stress

By

ERWIN N. GRISWOLD, M.A., LL.D., S.J.D.

NATHANIEL *1904* —

Dean and Langdell Professor of Law
Harvard Law School

HARVARD UNIVERSITY PRESS
CAMBRIDGE, MASSACHUSETTS
1965

©

Erwin N. Griswold

1964

Second printing 1965

Printed in the United States of America

PREFACE

THE material in this book was delivered as the Hamlyn Lectures in England in the fall of 1964. The purpose of this lectureship is to increase the knowledge of comparative jurisprudence among the common people of the United Kingdom in order that they "may realize the privileges which in law and custom they enjoy," and that "appreciating such privileges may recognize the responsibilities and obligations attaching to them."

In undertaking to give the lectures, I have sought to explain to an English audience some of the background of our legal system, and some of the problems with which we try to deal in that system. Many of these problems are commonplace to Americans. Yet, we may ourselves be so enmeshed in our own legal system that we are not fully aware of the complexities which it involves and the many problems which we have not yet resolved in the development of our law. Because a picture prepared for others may be of use to ourselves, it has seemed appropriate to arrange for the publication of the lectures in the United States as well as in England.

The author gratefully acknowledges research assistance which he has had from Peter J. Rothenberg and Jerome I. Chapman, both members of the class of 1964 at the Harvard

v

Law School.   He has also had valuable help from William L. Taylor, General Counsel of the United States Commission on Civil Rights, and from Jeffrey Albert, a member of the legal staff of the Commission, in checking material included in Chapter 5.   Finally, the author extends thanks to Mrs. Elisabeth Wahlen, who has typed the manuscript.

ERWIN N. GRISWOLD.

July 1964.

CONTENTS

viii   *Contents*

CHAPTER 1

INTRODUCTION

MY CHARGE, under the terms of the Hamlyn Trust, is to tell you about the blessings of your own legal system. Having been invited from another country, though, I assume that I was not chosen to talk about the law of England.

In this situation, I am planning to take up some selected aspects of the law of the United States, with a dual objective. This may serve to help you to have a better understanding of our legal system and its many problems; and it may, too, lead to the conclusion that you are indeed privileged to live under your own constitutional and legal system. For my discussion will show you many problems with which you have not had to deal; and your lives have been made simpler and easier because you are spared that task. Thus by talking about some aspects of the law and the legal system of the United States, I may indeed point towards the blessings of the law and legal system under which you live.

Before going further, let me put down some basic facts about the United States and its law which should serve as background for everything that I say. These are well known, but it is easy to overlook them in considering legal problems of the two countries. The first fact is that the United States is very large, both in area and population. And it is a very diverse and complex country. Its climate runs from the arctic in Alaska to the tropical in Florida and California. Its economy varies from the factory to the mine to the farm.

Its society varies from the urban to the small town to the wide open spaces. And, largely in consequence of this diversity, and of great importance, from the legal point of view, is the Federal nature of its governmental and legal system.

The United States is not one word. It is two. We are States which are United together. But first of all, in history and in law, we are States. There are fifty of our States, and the District of Columbia, and Puerto Rico, and various other places such as the Virgin Islands, and Guam. Altogether, there are some fifty-five or fifty-six different legal systems existing side by side in the United States. There are great similarities among them. For the most part, with you, they share the great heritage of the common law. But the law in each one of these legal systems varies, both statute law and common law. To know something about the law of the United States is to know vast amounts of detail, far beyond anything with which an English lawyer need be concerned.

Among other things, this means that the legal topic or set of problems known as the conflict of laws is of great importance to us, internally, in the United States. With us, the subject is never known as Private International Law, as it is sometimes called with you. It is always " conflict of laws," since it deals primarily with internal or domestic conflicts among the diverse legal systems within the United States. Some of our best thought and many of our free-flowing legal words have been expended on the problems of the conflict of laws, and we are still far from coming to any satisfactory or generally accepted solutions even for some of the everyday problems.

But in addition to the separate legal systems, there is also the United States itself, which has a legislature, and courts, and, within its sphere, a legal system. Thus, in every State, there is both State law and Federal law; and—which is usually even more surprising to the outsider—there are both State courts and Federal courts. The task of drawing the lines between the Federal and the State function is a very difficult one. This is one of our many problems of Constitutional Law which make most of your problems of Constitutional Law seem rather simple by comparison.

Thus the American lawyer has much *more* law to know than you have; and many of the questions he has to deal with are much more *complex* than most of yours. This leads to different functions for our lawyers in many ways, and a different outlook both as to the role of the lawyer and in the way the lawyer looks at law. These things are not simple to understand. But I hope that you will bear this basic factual difference in mind as you consider what I have to say about American law.

One more cautionary word is in order, I believe, at this point. As I have pointed out, the United States is geographically large, and it has perhaps the most complicated legal structure that has ever been devised and made effective in man's effort to govern himself. Anything can happen in the United States, good or bad; and most everything does. In judging the United States, it may sometimes be appropriate and helpful to think in statistical terms, as the natural scientists often do. We are all familiar with the probability curve, which starts off low, rises to a sharp peak, and then tapers off again on the other side. Although the extremes are most spectacular, and more likely to be recorded in the press, it is the peak that is truly significant. We must guard ourselves against jumping too easily to conclusions from the more sensational and " newsworthy " items. Instead, we should look to the essentials which lie beyond. It is only in this way that one can have a reasonably accurate understanding of what is significant in the United States.

If you derive from this the conclusion that you are indeed blessed with your own legal system, I shall not be surprised. You may feel, too, that James Fitzjames Stephen was right when he asked in 1873 [1] whether " the enormous development of equality in America, the rapid production of an immense multitude of commonplace self-satisfied, and essentially slight people is an exploit which the world need fall down and worship." But I shall have complied with the terms of the trust which brought me here.

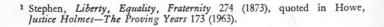

[1] Stephen, *Liberty, Equality, Fraternity* 274 (1873), quoted in Howe, *Justice Holmes—The Proving Years* 173 (1963).

CHAPTER 2

THE LEGAL PROFESSION IN THE UNITED STATES

STATISTICS

ACCORDING to the latest figures, there are now more than 296,000 lawyers in the United States. Of these, a few more than 200,000 are engaged in the private practice of law. The rest are in government service, employed by business corporations, in full-time law teaching, or are retired.

In order to give the full picture, the current tabulation which has been made by Martindale-Hubbell, Inc., the publishers of our standard legal directory, is set out here:

	1964
Lawyers accounted for	296,069
In private practice	
Individual	113,127
Partner	70,064
Associate	17,395
Total	200,586
Government service	29,314
Salaried in industry	26,492
Educational (salaried)	2,100
Other private employment	918
Inactive or retired	12,024
Women lawyers	7,143

The comparison with the situation in England is rather striking. As I understand it, there are about 20,000 solicitors in England, and 4,000 members of the bar, of whom perhaps

2,000 are engaged in practice. Thus, though the population of the United States is nearly 4 times that of the United Kingdom, it has more than 10 times as many lawyers. This means that there are at least two and a half times as many lawyers per capita in the United States as there are in the United Kingdom. Are we more litigious? Apparently we are—but why? Or is it that our law is more complicated, that our lawyers have more office work to do, or, perhaps, that our lawyers are less efficient in handling legal work? I cannot give specific answers to these questions, but I hope in these lectures to present to you some of the data which may bear upon the answers.

At the outset, I should say that I cannot paint a picture of the legal profession in the United States which shows it as near perfection as is the legal profession in England as described by Mr. Megarry in his Hamlyn lectures of two years ago. I am willing to accept that here " God's in his Heaven, and all's right with the world." With us, God is indeed in his Heaven, but He has left much more for us to do. Your legal profession is, of course, the product of your history and social conditions, and it is greatly admired wherever it is known. Our history and social conditions have been quite different, and our problems have by no means been wholly resolved.

Thus, it is appropriate to begin this discussion of the American legal profession with a summary of the history of lawyers in the United States. Following this, I will outline the position and organization of American lawyers at the present time. Then, having seen where we are and how we got there, I shall try to indicate where we may be going, by pointing out some of the significant problems facing our profession today.

HISTORY

Let us start out by taking a quick look at the history of the legal profession in the United States.[1]

The Early Days

The American colonies were settled in the first part of the seventeenth century. But each one had a quite different history. For many years there was little direct contact between them. And to a considerable extent, there was little connection with the Mother country. Many of the colonists were refugees. They left England because they wanted to get away from something they did not like here. For the most part, they had little use for the law of England, and they felt virtually no need for lawyers. The reasons varied from place to place. For example, in New York, this may have been due to the desire of the merchants to keep things in their own hands. In Pennsylvania, it was due to the influence of the Quakers.

In Massachusetts, the early government was a theocracy. Laws were based upon the Bible, and doubtful points were resolved by divines, and not by lawyers. The earliest code of laws in Massachusetts, known as the Body of Liberties, was

---

[1] In the passages which follow, I have drawn freely on several well known works dealing with the history of lawyers in America. These are: Warren, *A History of the American Bar* (1911), which is the basic source of information; Reed, *Training for the Public Profession of the Law* (1921); Pound, *The Lawyer from Antiquity to Modern Times* (1953); Chroust, "The Legal Profession in Colonial America," 33 *Notre Dame Lawyer* 51, 350 (1957, 1958), 34 *Notre Dame Lawyer* 44 (1958); Chroust, "The Dilemma of the American Lawyer in the Post-Revolutionary Era," 35 *Notre Dame Lawyer* 48 (1959). See also Stone, "The Lawyer and His Neighbors," 4 *Cornell L.Q.* 175 (1919); Blackard, "Requirements for Admission to the Bar in Revolutionary America," 15 *Tenn.L.Rev.* 116 (1938); Blackard, "The Demoralization of the Legal Profession in Nineteenth Century America," 16 *Tenn.L.Rev.* 314 (1940).

drafted by two Puritan ministers, the Rev. John Cotton and the Rev. Nathaniel Ward. Ward had been a barrister of Lincoln's Inn before he became a minister. Their code provided that wherever the law did not cover a matter, decision was to be made according to "the word of God."[2] Under such a system, there was no place for lawyers. Later in the century some persons were admitted as attorneys, but as late as 1700 there was no person in Massachusetts who had been trained for the law.

By this time, the theocratic basis of the legal system had declined, and with the coming of the eighteenth century a few more lawyers appear on the scene. How they were trained, or whether they were trained at all, does not appear. We do know that by the middle of the eighteenth century there were a number of lawyers, and that the custom had developed that a young man who wanted to follow the law would associate himself for a period of years with an experienced practitioner. As there were no offices or chambers, this often meant that the younger man would go to live with the older one in his home, as John Adams did in the home of James Putnam of Worcester, in 1755. By this time a number of men from Massachusetts had been trained at the Inns of Court. The first of these was Benjamin Lynde, who entered the Middle Temple in 1692, and later became Chief Justice of Massachusetts. Paul Dudley, his successor as Chief Justice, was called to the bar of the Inner Temple in 1700. Two generations later, John Gardner was admitted to the Inner

---

[2] See generally Haskins, *Law and Authority in Early Massachusetts* (1960); Miller, *Orthodoxy in Massachusetts, 1630–1659* (1933). *Cf.* Eusden, *Puritans, Lawyers and Politics in Early Seventeenth Century England* (1958).

Temple in 1761. All of these persons had gone to Harvard College, which by this time had done much to produce an educated group in the Massachusetts Province.

The Eighteenth Century

During the eighteenth century there was a steady growth both in the number of lawyers and in their influence, in all of the colonies. As shown in the legal papers of John Adams, soon to be published, there were outstanding lawyers in this era, and they conducted their affairs in substantially the same way as do the leading lawyers of the present day.[3] A considerable number of young men studied in England. From 1760 to the close of the American Revolution, 115 Americans were admitted to the Inns of Court. More than a third of these, or 47, came from South Carolina; 21 came from Virginia; 16 from Maryland; 11 from Pennsylvania[4]; 5 from New York; and 1 or 2 from each of the other colonies. Most of the legal education, however, was apprentice education.

Some elements of a separation in the profession may be found. Those who had been called to the bar in England were regarded as barristers. Those who were trained by other lawyers at home were admitted as attorneys. This admission was by the court, as was the practice in the admission of attorneys in England. But after an attorney had practiced in the inferior courts for two years, he could become a counselor; and after two years more he could become a barrister.

---

[3] See Wroth and Zobel, *The Legal Papers of John Adams*, documents Nos. 44, 46, 63, 64 (to be published in 1965).

[4] See Nolan, '' Pennsylvania Students at the Inns of Court,'' No. 2 *Pa.Bar Ass'n Q.* 22 (1929).

Barristers wore gowns and wigs. Writing of the setting
for James Otis' famous argument against Writs of Assistance
in Massachusetts in 1761, John Adams observed that the
judges wore "immense judicial wiggs" and that all the
barristers of the neighbourhood were there "in their Gowns,
Bands and Tye Wiggs." [5]

Similarly a portrait of Andrew Hamilton, a lawyer of
Pennsylvania, famous for his defense of John Peter Zenger,
shows him dressed in "a long flowing wig, a scarlet coat,
frilled bosom, and *bands*, precisely like those worn by some
denominations of the clergy . . ." [6]

This use of distinguishing titles apparently continued for
some years after the Revolution. In Virginia, there was an
upper and lower bar until 1787. In Pennsylvania, there was
a lower bar on a local basis; and Georgia had a higher bar,
the members of which alone could be heard in the appellate
courts. The first rules of the United States Supreme Court,
issued in 1790, before the Court had any business, provided
that counselors could not practice as attorneys, and that
attorneys could not practice as counselors. This restriction
was eliminated in 1801.

Despite the variations in titles of members of the legal
profession, there never seems to have been a clear separation
in function. Although a counselor or barrister might devote
most of his professional time to court appearances, he was not
confined to that sort of activity. Nor was he required to be

---

[5] Letter from John Adams to William Tudor, to be published in *The Legal
Papers of John Adams*, document No. 44 (editorial note). See also
Adams, *Diary and Autobiography*, vol. 3, 276 (Butterfield ed. 1961);
Warren, *The Supreme Court in United States History*, vol. 1, 48 (Rev.
ed. 1932), which shows that the Justices of the United States Supreme
Court at first wore scarlet robes and wigs, but soon discarded them.

[6] The portrait is so described in Brown, *The Forum*, vol. 1, 243 (1856).

briefed by an attorney. He was quite free to deal directly with his clients, and ordinarily did so. It is not surprising, in this situation, that the entire group of practitioners came to be called " the bar," even though only a few of them had literally been called to the bar by one of the Inns of Court in England. The word " solicitor " never came into use in the United States as applying to a legal practitioner; and the term " barrister " gradually went out of use as the custom of going to the Inns of Court ceased. Thus, in the course of time, lawyers in the United States came to be known as "Attorneys and Counselors at Law." That is what appears on many letterheads and office doors to this day. And collectively, they came to be known as members of the bar. With us, any lawyer is a member of the bar, though he is " admitted " by a court, and not "called " by an Inn or guild of lawyers. In the process we have inevitably lost much of professional feeling and solidarity; and we have also lost much of discipline and control. To English ears, it must sound pretentious when we all call ourselves " members of the bar," and when the American Bar Association descends on you in droves as it does from time to time. But to us, it is simply the natural use of the term. Though we are all members of the bar because we have been admitted to the bar by our respective courts, we do not think of ourselves as barristers. With us, that term has largely dropped out of use except as a literary term, or in reference to the English bar.

The Effects of the Revolution

The American lawyer reached a peak at the time of the Revolution. Twenty-five of the 56 signers of the Declaration of Independence were lawyers; and, at the close of the revolutionary period, 31 of the 55 members of the Constitutional Convention of 1787 were lawyers. Of the latter group 5 had studied in England. But the ranks of American lawyers were greatly weakened as a result of the Revolution, as many lawyers took the loyalist side, and either left the country, or ceased to practice. When the British evacuated Boston, at least 12 Massachusetts lawyers went to Halifax, or left for other places outside the country. These included Samuel Fitch, Benjamin Gridley, and also John Adams' preceptor, James Putnam. Judge Washburn has told us that there were 36 barristers and 10 attorneys in Boston in 1775.[7] Those who left numbered a third to a fourth of the total. No figures appear to be available for the other colonies, but one list gives a total of 48 lawyers who left, from various parts of the country.[8] There is no doubt that this was a serious set-back to the over-all caliber of the profession in America.

For many years after the Revolution there was, as might be expected, a strong hostility to things English, including English law. During the course of the Revolution, this view was expressed by a pamphleteer in terms which also show the hostility to lawyers which was a part of this attitude:

"One reason of the pernicious practice of the law and what gives great influence to the 'order' is that we have introduced the whole body of English law into our courts. Why should these States be governed by British laws? Can the monarchical and aristocratical institutions of England be

[7] Washburn, *Sketches of the Judicial History of Massachusetts from 1630 to 1775*, at 200–201 (1840).
[8] Sabine, *Biographical Sketches of Loyalists of the American Revolution,* vol. 2 (1864).

consistent with the republican principles of our Constitution? . . . The numerous precedents brought from 'old English authorities' . . . answer no other purpose than to increase the influence of lawyers." [9]

New Jersey enacted a statute making it an offense for a lawyer to cite in court any decision, opinion, treatise, compilation or exposition of the common law which had appeared after July 1, 1776.[10] Similar statutes were passed in Pennsylvania [11] and Kentucky.[12] An extreme instance of this view is recorded in a charge given to a jury by John Dudley, a judge of the New Hampshire Supreme Court, though not a lawyer. He is reported to have said:

> "Gentlemen, you have heard what has been said in this case by the lawyers, the rascals! . . . They talk of law. Why, gentlemen, it is not law that we want, but justice! They would govern us by the common law of England. Common-sense is a much safer guide. . . . A clear head and an honest heart are worth more than all the law of all the lawyers. . . . It is our duty to do justice between the parties, not by any quirks of the law out of Coke and Blackstone,— books that I never read and never will." [13]

[9] Honestus (Benjamin Austin), "Observations on the Pernicious Practice of the Law," published in the Independent Chronicle of Boston in 1786, quoted in Warren, *A History of the American Bar* 228 (1911).

[10] N.J. Acts of June 13, 1799, sec. 5; Patterson, *Laws of New Jersey* 436.

[11] Pa. Act of March 19, 1810, Pa.Pub. Laws 136 (1810). This was repealed in 1836. Pa. Act of March 29, 1836, Pa.Pub. Laws 224 (1836).

[12] Ky. Act of Feb. 12, 1808, Digest of the Statute Law of Ky., vol. 1, tit. 70, p. 613 (1834). Henry Clay was stopped from reading from 3 *East's Reports. Hickman* v. *Boffin*, 1 Hardin 356, 372 (Ky. 1808).

[13] Corning, "The Highest Courts of Law in New Hampshire—Colonial, Provincial and State," 2 *Green Bag* 469, 471 (1890). See also 40 *Am.L. Rev.* 436 (1906).

Anglophobic

14 14   *The Legal Profession in the United States*

At this time there were no American law books,[14] and
virtually no reported American decisions. The first volume
of reports was published in 1789. This was Kirby's Reports,
covering decisions in Connecticut from 1785 to 1788. In the
next ten years, a few more volumes of reports were published
—Root's Reports (Connecticut), in two volumes, Dallas
(Pennsylvania), Chipman (Vermont), Wythe (Virginia), and
Martin (North Carolina). By 1820, there were less than
200 volumes of American law reports.[15] In this situation,
whether frowned on or not, there was little alternative but
recourse to Blackstone. The American edition of Blackstone
was published in 1771, and more copies were sold, it is said,
than were sold of the edition published in England. Thus,
Blackstone was, for many years the chief link with English
law. It was fortunate, indeed, that his lectures were delivered
just prior to the revolutionary period, so that they escaped the
worst of the Anglophobic restrictions. Their influence on
our law has been incalculable.

" The Golden Age "

Despite the stumbling blocks of the post-revolutionary era
and despite the unpopularity resulting from the fact that most
of the business available to lawyers at the time was debt
collection, the legal profession managed to hold a special

---

[14] " In the hundred years between the publication in 1687 of William Penn's
gleanings from Lord Coke and the issuance of the American editions of
Buller's *Nisi Prius* and Gilbert's *Evidence* in 1788, not a single book that
could be called a treatise intended for the use of professional lawyers was
published in the British Colonies and the American States." James, " A
List of Legal Treatises Printed in the British Colonies and the American
States before 1801," *Harvard Legal Essays* 159 (1934).

[15] Reed, *Training for the Public Profession of the Law* 374 (1921).

position in early nineteenth century America. The most acute observer of the United States in that period, Alexis de Toqueville, remarked:

> "In America there are no nobles or literary men, and the people are apt to mistrust the wealthy; lawyers consequently form the highest political class and the most cultivated circle of society. . . . If I were asked where I place the American Aristocracy, I should reply without hesitation, that it is not composed of the rich, who are united by no common tie, but that it occupies the judicial bench and the bar." [16]

In Dean Pound's language, the first half of the nineteenth century was the "Golden Age" of American Law.[17] It is undeniable that there were great figures in that period: Marshall and Story on the bench, and Webster, Clay, and Reverdy Johnson at the bar, among others. But generally speaking, the position of the bar deteriorated rapidly.

"Deprofessionalizing"

As early as 1790 Massachusetts had passed an act under which any person, whether he was a lawyer or not, might appear in court on behalf of another. All he needed was the written power of attorney of the person for whom he was appearing.[18] This statute remained in effect until the 1930's and was the basis on which the Harvard Legal Aid Bureau was able to function, with student counsel, in its early years. But it was, also, within my own experience in Massachusetts,

---

[16] de Toqueville, *Democracy in America,* vol. 2, 184-85 (2d ed. 1836).

[17] Pound, *The Lawyer from Antiquity to Modern Times* 185 (1953). See generally Pound, *The Formative Era in American Law* (1938).

[18] Mass. Laws and Resolves 1789, ch. 58; included in Mass. Gen. Laws, ch. 221, sec. 49 (Ter. ed. 1932). Repealed by Mass. Acts & Resolves 1935, ch. 346, sec. 3.

a means by which disbarred lawyers continued to appear in court on behalf of clients, not as attorneys at law, but as attorneys in fact.

Increased impetus for this sort of legislation came with the flowering of Jacksonian democracy in the second third of the nineteenth century. This overzealous democratization may well be said to be the chief cause of the major problems which have confronted the law and the legal profession in the United States down to the present day. Two prime factors underlie what has been called the "deprofessionalizing" [19] of the American bar in the 1840's. First, there was the phenomenon of the versatile and self-sufficient frontiersman. Frequently being in no position to call upon others for help, he learned to do everything for himself. Soon he came to regard himself as qualified to perform any service, and he assumed that other responsible citizens possessed the same comprehensive abilities. Secondly, there was the great influence of the natural law concept. In its extreme form, this led beyond the view that every citizen was equal to every other and encompassed the idea that every citizen had a natural right to follow any business, profession or calling.

Under such influence, the legislature of Massachusetts provided in 1836 that if a man was of good moral character and had read law for three years in an attorney's office, the courts were required to admit him. This Act remained in force for forty years. But it was surpassed in a few years by laws in a number of states which eliminated the educational qualification altogether. Thus, in 1842 New Hampshire provided that every citizen over twenty-one years of age might practice

[19] Pound, *The Lawyer from Antiquity to Modern Times* 232 (1953).

law.[20] In 1843 Maine enacted that every citizen might be a lawyer.[21] In Wisconsin, after 1849, it was every resident.[22] In Indiana, a provision was put into the constitution of the state in 1851 which read: "Every person of good moral character, being a voter, shall be entitled to admission to practice law in all courts of justice."

The subsequent history of this provision is instructive. Numerous efforts to get the provision amended out of the State Constitution were unsuccessful. In 1881, however, a statute was passed authorizing the courts to set an optional examination in legal learning, and to enter the names of successful applicants upon a special roll. Where a candidate for admission refused to waive his right to be examined only as to his moral character, the court could require him to prove his character before a jury, thus giving publicity to his refusal.

In 1893, the Supreme Court of Indiana held that a woman of good moral character was entitled to practice law in the State, even though she was not a voter, and at that time could not become a voter. In the course of its opinion in this case, the court voiced the "natural right" view which was deep-seated in American thinking. It said: "Whatever the objections of the common law of England, there is a law higher in this country, and better suited to the rights and liberties of American citizens, that law which accords to every citizen the natural right to gain a livelihood by intelligence, honesty and industry in the arts, the sciences, the professions, or other vocations." [23]

[20] N.H. Rev. Stat. 1842, ch. 177, sec. 2.
[21] Maine Acts & Resolves 1843, ch. 12.
[22] Wis. Rev. Stat. 1849, ch. 87, sec. 26.
[23] *In re Petition of Leach*, 134 Ind. 665, 668, 34 N.E. 641, 642 (1893).

But by 1928, the approach had shifted. In that year the then Supreme Court of Indiana went out of its way to say that " the practice of the law in this State is not an unqualified constitutional or natural right. It should be termed a privilege." [24] Finally, in 1932, by a popular referendum vote, the constitutional provision was at last repealed, and Indiana now has a bar examination like every other State. (Parenthetically, I may state that my grandfather was a resident and voter in Indiana from about 1851 until 1922, and he never sought to practice law there, natural and constitutional rights to do so notwithstanding.)

Even in more recent times, some State legislatures have sought to intervene in matters of bar admissions. In 1925, and in 1933, the legislature of Tennessee passed Acts providing that a person, named in each Act, who had not passed the bar examination, should be admitted to the practice of law.[25] In 1939, such Acts were held invalid by the Tennessee Supreme Court.[26] An even more striking instance occurred in Wisconsin at about the same time. A lawyer named Cannon was suspended from the practice of law for two years by order of the Supreme Court, after hearing on a charge of unlawful solicitation of business, collecting excessive fees, and improper conduct toward the bench and his fellow lawyers. The legislature then passed an Act which undertook to restore him to membership in the bar.[27] The court held the statute invalid, though it did, as an exercise of its own discretion,

---

[24] *In re McDonald,* 200 Ind. 424, 428, 164 N.E. 261, 262 (1928).
[25] Tenn. Pub. Acts 1925, ch. 73; Tenn. Pub. Acts 1933, ch. 180.
[26] *Lineburger* v. *State, ex rel. Beeler,* 174 Tenn. 538, 129 S.W.2d 198 (1939). See also 16 *Tenn.L.Rev.* 239 (1940).
[27] Wis. Acts 1931, ch. 480.

and apart from the statute, enter an order reinstating him.[28]

The principal basis on which such decisions are rested is that of separation of powers, derived from French thinking of the eighteenth century and forming the underlying assumption of all of our Constitutions. Admission to the bar has now come to be held to be a purely judicial function into which the legislature may not enter, except perhaps to establish procedures designed to assist the court in the exercise of its responsibility.[29]

The democratic zeal that marked the second third of the nineteenth century had its effect not only on the bar but upon the bench as well. This same era brought us the election of judges beginning in Mississippi in 1832, and spreading to a total of 38 States. Also in this era came denial to our judges of any right to comment on the evidence in a jury trial. In some States, the judge charges the jury before counsel make their closing arguments or summations, and in many States, the judge may not charge the jury except in terms which are proposed by counsel. The charge must either be given as written by counsel, or refused by the judge as a matter of law. This makes judges in many of our States little more than passive umpires or moderators, leaving to counsel any truly significant active role in the trial of a case.

The period we have been discussing naturally led to a great " demoralization of the legal profession." [30] Much of it must leave English ears incredulous. But it is a stark reality

[28] *In re Cannon,* 206 Wis. 374, 240 N.W. 441 (1932). There is a discussion of the matter in 17 *A.B.A.J.* 561, 594 (1931).

[29] See Opinion of the Justices, 279 Mass. 607, 180 N.E. 725 (1932); *Olmstead's Case,* 292 Pa. 96, 140 Atl. 634 (1928).

[30] Blackard, " The Demoralization of the Legal Profession in Nineteenth Century America," 16 *Tenn.L.Rev.* 314 (1941).

in our history. As Dean Pound has said, "The harm which this deprofessionalizing of the practice of law did to the law, to legal procedure, to the ethics of practice and to forensic conduct has outlived the era in which it took place and still presents problems to the promoters of more effective administration of justice." And, he adds, "The opposition to an educated, adequately trained Bar and to an independent, experienced, permanent Judiciary . . . left a mark upon our law and procedure which we have been striving hard to erase in the present century." [31]

All of these developments are deplorable in my opinion. The wonder, though, is that we have done as well as we have in modifying or alleviating them. You are fortunate in the United Kingdom that you have been spared such excesses of democratic zeal. In evaluating lawyers and the legal process in the United States, you should make allowance for these special problems with which we must constantly deal, and which necessarily color our legal thinking and affect our professional actions.

Modern Organization of the Profession

Until 1870, there were only the barest beginnings of any effective organizations for lawyers in the United States. Lawyers were scattered widely over dozens of States and hundreds of cities and towns, with no centralized body such as the Inns of Court, or the Law Society, exercising any sort of control or leadership, and with little or no standards of legal education or of admission to the bar. It can be said that the low point was reached about 1870. That we have made

[31] Pound, *The Lawyer from Antiquity to Modern Times* 232, 237 (1953).

Tilden

as much progress as we have since that time is due to the
devoted thought and effort of thousands of lawyers throughout
the country.

There were associations of lawyers for the purpose of providing library facilities in a number of cities from a very early
time, and the Philadelphia Bar Association can trace its
history back to 1802. Indeed, that Association did much to
maintain standards in that city, and may even have played a
part in the origin of the phrase "a Philadelphia lawyer,"
which is sometimes used to mean a lawyer of uncommon
energy and ability. But the modern history of bar associations
in the United States starts with the organization of the
Association of the Bar of the City of New York in 1870,
under the leadership of Samuel J. Tilden. The Association
was organized in large part to help to combat the corrupt
ring of Boss Tweed which was then dominating the city. In
this objective, the Association of the Bar proved successful.
Since that time it has grown and developed, until I think it
can fairly be said to be the leading organization of lawyers
in the United States. It maintains a fine house in uptown
New York, with one of the great law libraries in the country.
Notable among its dozens of active standing committees are
the Committee on Grievances, which investigates charges
against lawyers and initiates disciplinary proceedings where
appropriate, and the Committee on the Judiciary, which is
charged with making recommendations as to the qualifica-
tions of candidates for election as judges. This committee's
reports are considered by the Association at open meetings,
and appropriate publicity is given to the Association's final
recommendations. In addition, the Association has established
many special committees, whose research studies on matters

of great public importance in the legal area have frequently spurred beneficial changes in legislation and in administrative practices.[32]   The Association, while limited for its active membership to lawyers from New York City, has many associate members in all parts of the country. Thus its special committees often have representatives from many different places, and the matters considered are not confined to those of interest in New York only.

The activities of the Association of the Bar of the City of New York are not always solemn and serious ones. It has a social and cultural program which helps to broaden the interests of its members and to develop something of a corporate feeling among them. Much of this phase of its activities goes back to the interest and efforts of Harrison Tweed (not related to Boss Tweed), who was President of the Association just after the late war. A passage from his inaugural address is now carved on a plaque in one of the principal meeting rooms of the Association (and also at the Harvard Law School). It reads as follows [33]:

> "I have a high opinion of lawyers. With all their faults, they stack up well against those in every other occupation or profession. They are better to work with or play with or fight with or drink with, than most other varieties of mankind."

[32] See, for example, the following reports, all by Special Committees of the Association of the Bar of the City of New York: *Children and Families in the Courts of New York City*, including a study by Walter Gellhorn (1954); *Bad Housekeeping: The Administration of the New York Courts* (1955); *The Federal Loyalty-Security Program* (1956); *Impartial Medical Testimony* (1956); *Equal Justice for the Accused* (1959); *Conflict of Interest and Federal Service* (1960); *Mental Illness and Due Process*, with Cornell Law School (1962); *Who Sues in New York City,* with Columbia Law School (1962).

[33] 1 *Record of N.Y.C.B.A.* 8 (1946).

American Bar Association

The American Bar Association, our first National organization of lawyers, was organized at Saratoga Springs, New York, in 1878. At first, and for many years, its objectives were chiefly social, and it was a rather exclusive organization, open only to those who were regarded as leaders of the bar in their communities. This meant, among other things, that it had a very conservative outlook, as the leaders of the bar in our country are likely to be those who represent wealthy individuals or big corporations, and they tend to share the interests of these clients, who, until very recently, at least, did not look with favor on changes in the status quo.

After 25 years, in 1903, the American Bar Association had 2,000 members. Ten years later, in 1913, it had 8,000 members. In 1928, after 50 years, it had 28,000 members. In 1950 its membership was 42,000. Not long after that, it ceased to be especially exclusive and sought memberships from lawyers throughout the country. This has resulted in a great increase in membership, so that the Association now has 115,000 members, which is close to half of all of the active lawyers in the country.

But the American Bar Association remains a voluntary organization; and though it has considerable influence in many fields, it has no real powers over any member of the profession. The most that it can do in the way of discipline is to suspend or expel a member, but this does not affect his right to practice law. The Association's Canons of Ethics are widely looked to, and have been adopted in many of the States. And the opinions of its Committee on Ethics have great influence.[34] But it might be fair to say that they have

---

[34] See generally Drinker, *Legal Ethics* (1953).

influence on the lawyers who would not break the Canons anyway, and that the lawyers whose ethical practices are more doubtful rarely become members of the Association.

The Association is now so big that it has necessarily become quite cumbersome. Some 5,000 or 6,000 lawyers attend its Annual Meetings; and the total attendance including wives and families now runs to 10,000 or 12,000 persons, so that there are few cities which have hotel facilities adequate to handle the meetings. But the average member has little opportunity to take part in the policy making activities of the Association. An effort to deal with this problem was made in 1936, when the structure of the Association was completely reorganized. At that time, final power to speak for the Association was placed in a House of Delegates, which now numbers about 300 members. One of these from each State is elected by a mail ballot of the Association members in that State, for a three year term. He is known as the State Delegate. Then there are members representing State and local bar associations, the various Sections of the American Bar Association, certain affiliated associations, and some public officers, such as the Attorney General and the Solicitor General of the United States. The House of Delegates ordinarily meets twice a year, for three or four days at a time. Its deliberations and consideration are usually on a high level, and in recent years especially there has been a marked tendency to consider matters from a broad point of view not unduly influenced by the interests of clients.

Apart from the main body of the American Bar Association, its members have the opportunity of belonging to any one or more of its many Sections. These deal with such matters as Labor Law, Administrative Law, Real Property, Probate and Trust Law, Tax Law, Antitrust Law, and Business or Corporate Law. Much of the most effective work of the Association is done in these Sections. I have been a member of the Tax Section since its organization about 1940, and many of my best and most enjoyable professional associations have come from this work.

In an organization as large as the American Bar Association, with members from every part of the country, every point of view is strongly represented. But as you know, many questions in American life are deeply controversial. Where opinions are sharply divided, probably no single Association point of view ought to be announced, even though a majority of votes can be mustered for one side or the other. Some ten years or so ago, under the leadership of some vigorous but ultra-conservative presidents, the Association did take some positions which seemed to me to be very unfortunate, unsound, and backward looking. Because of such actions as these, many of my friends and colleagues would not become members of the Association. It has always seemed to me that this is quite wrong. If all of the people who would like to see constructive actions and progress stay out of the Association, it can hardly be expected that its actions will be anything but extremely conservative. The thing to do, it seems to me, is to join the Association, and work to improve its outlook. Besides, for better or for worse, it is the one great National organization of lawyers in our country. We are a profession, and we are more likely to become an effective profession if we work together on our common professional problems.

Other National Associations

Along with the American Bar Association are a number of other organizations. One of these, the American Judicature Society, was organized in 1913 for the purpose of improving the administration of justice in the United States. Over the years it has worked for better methods of selecting judges, and it developed the plan, now often called the Missouri Plan, under which judges are appointed by the Governor of the State from names provided him by a panel set up for the purpose. The person so named serves as a judge for a short term, and then has to submit himself to the voters on a ballot which simply says: Shall so-and-so be retained in office? There is no contest with any other person, and if the judge is then retained he gets a fairly long term, and may be re-elected at the end of that term on the same basis, subject to retirement provisions for age. This plan retains the form of election, but provides much of the advantages of appointment. It is used in California as well as in Missouri, and in some other States. If it could become more widely adopted, we might be able to move farther away from the system of elected judges with which we were saddled by our fathers a century and a quarter ago.

Another organization is the American Law Institute, established more than forty years ago, and now consisting of 1,500 lawyer members. The Institute is responsible for the publication of the Restatements of the Law, which have done much to organize and systematize our chaotic system of varying State laws. The Restatements have no authoritative standing, but they do have considerable influence when novel points come up in the several States. In recent years, the Institute has also drafted some model codes for consideration by State legislatures. These include a Model Code of Evidence, and more recently a Model Penal Code. The Institute has proved itself to be a useful meeting place for the thoughtful practitioners and the academic lawyers in fruitful cooperative work in improving the law.

Finally, there is the National Conference of Commissioners on Uniform State Laws, an official body, with three delegates from each State. It is engaged in preparing drafts of Uniform Statutes for submission to the State legislatures, in the hope that some of our law may be made more uniform throughout the United States. The Commissioners have done good work, and have drafted a considerable number of excellent laws. But it is extremely difficult to persuade the legislatures to enact these laws.

In some sixty-five years of existence, only one of these statutes was enacted in every State. This was the Uniform Negotiable Instruments Law, patterned somewhat on the Bills of Exchange Act here. This has now been superseded, however, by the Uniform Commercial Code, on which work was completed about 1953. This Code was a joint product of the Commissioners on Uniform State Laws and the American Law Institute. It has now been enacted in some thirty States, and it is hoped that in due course it will be enacted by all fifty of the States, by Congress for the District of Columbia, and perhaps by Congress so far as it affects interstate commerce.

The amount of time and effort which are required to secure enactment of one of these laws by some fifty-two or -three jurisdictions is almost unbelievable. It is some index to the problem of effective law development and reform in the United States. Even when a Uniform Law is involved, some of the legislatures feel free to make amendments. Thus, when the Uniform Commercial Code was enacted in California, the legislature there made some two hundred amendments. Some of these may possibly have been improvements in an abstract sense, but they were bought at a high cost to the objective of uniformity, which must be maintained if these enactments are really to be effective on a nationwide basis.

State and Local Bar Associations

In addition to these National organizations, there is an organization of the bar in every State, and also a separate organization in most of the cities of the country. Many of these associations do effective work. A few of them, as in Ohio, Michigan, and Wisconsin, have substantial buildings, and are beginning to conduct effective research activities. Some of the State and local associations are primarily social organizations. I do not deprecate the social activity at all, as camaraderie among the lawyers is one of the elements of a profession. As is always the case in the United States, there is no way to generalize about the State and local associations. They vary from extremely good to mediocre and ineffective. I think it can be said that nearly all of them are now much better than they were a generation ago.

Beginning about forty years ago there was a considerable movement in the United States towards an "integrated" bar in the States, and about twenty of the States now have an integrated bar, either pursuant to a statute or by an order of the State Supreme Court. When the bar is integrated, all lawyers must belong. They must maintain their annual membership to keep up their license to practice, and they become subject to the disciplinary action of the State Bar.

There is much to be said in favor of integration of the bar, and this has been persuasive in a number of States. Yet, in other States, compulsory membership is rather fiercely resisted, In those States, such as my own State of Massachusetts, many of the individual practitioners want to maintain their own complete individuality, and to refrain from any sort of corporate affiliation at all. As one result, we do not even know how many lawyers there are in Massachusetts; and this is true, too, in most of the other States which do not have an integrated bar. In such States the bar associations remain entirely voluntary, and have no effective powers over their members, except to drop them from membership. They can also institute proceedings in court looking towards disciplinary action against any lawyer, but they cannot take such action themselves.

CURRENT PROBLEMS

Having reviewed the history and organization of the American legal profession, I would like to touch briefly upon some major problems of the relation of American lawyers among themselves and to the populace they serve. Thought and study about these problems are only just beginning in our country.

Professional Stratification

Although the profession in the United States is not formally divided, as it is in England, between attorneys and barristers, several recent studies dramatically point out that "over the past sixty years, a highly stratified bar has evolved in urban America." [35] Throughout the nineteenth century,

---

[35] Ladinsky, "The Impact of Social Backgrounds of Lawyers on Law Practice and the Law," 16 *J.Leg.Ed*. 127 (1963).

FIRMS

the individual practitioner prevailed; in 1872, there was one law firm in New York City with six partners, and in 1900, there were only two firms with as many as nine partners.[36] But large firms grew rapidly in the present century. Several New York firms now have over 100 lawyers, and there are at least 23 firms with over 50 lawyers outside of New York. As of 1958, 52% of all lawyers were in practice for themselves, 28% were practicing in firms, and the rest were employed by government or corporations, or were judges or teachers.[37] As indicated by the figures given at the beginning of this Chapter, the proportion practicing in firms is slowly increasing.

Behind the statistics of this stratification lie real differences in background and in quality and kind of legal work. A study based on a sample of 207 lawyers in Detroit, Michigan, reveals that individual practitioners " more often come from working class and entrepreneurial families of minority religious and ethnic status." [38] It also appears that the solo lawyers, on average, have had quantitatively less and qualitatively inferior education than the firm lawyers. Finally, the Detroit figures show a considerable though not overwhelming variation in incomes between the solo and the firm practitioners. Of the lone practitioners, 21% made less than $10,000 a year, while only 10% of the firm lawyers were in this bracket. On the other hand, only 18% of the solo practitioners made more than $30,000 a year as compared with 38% of the firm lawyers who were in this category.

---

[36] Koegel, *Walter S. Carter, Collector of Young Masters* 7 (1955).
[37] American Bar Foundation, *Lawyers in the United States: Distribution and Income*, 1958 Supplement, at 54–55 (1959).
[38] Ladinsky, " The Impact of Social Backgrounds of Lawyers on Law Practice and the Law," 16 *J.Leg.Ed.* 127, 130 (1963).

Just what conclusions should be drawn from information such as this is far from clear. For example, the figures, being confined to lawyers in active practice, either solo or in firms, make no allowance for the many lawyers who are in various forms of public service, employed by business corporations, in law teaching, in politics, or indeed, on the bench. It may well be that these other lines of endeavor provide considerable opportunities for members of minority groups. Moreover, there are variations in the abilities and interests and tempera- ments of individuals, and it is natural and predictable that some will work more effectively in some circumstances than in others. Some may have elected solo practice, knowing that it would be financially less rewarding, because of the independence and satisfaction which it brings.

A revealing look at the lot of the solo practitioner was presented in a recent study of 84 lawyers practicing by them- selves in Chicago. The author concludes that "the lawyer practicing by himself is generally at the bottom of the status ladder of the metropolitan bar." He "is most likely to be found at the margin of his profession, enjoying little freedom in choice of clients, type of work, or conditions of practice." He is "rarely called upon to exercise a high level of pro- fessional skill." The individual practitioners in some big cities are heavily concentrated in certain ethnic groups. For example, at least 68 percent of the lawyers considered had one parent born abroad, and the ethnic background of 53 per- cent was in eastern Europe.[39] Many of these lawyers had

---

[39] Carlin, *Lawyers on Their Own* 24 (1962), reviewed in 16 *J.Leg.Ed.* 376 (1964).

gone to law school in the 1930's, when educational standards were lower than they are now. Sixty-seven percent of them had gone to part-time law schools.

These differences do not obtain only between firm and single practitioners; among the law firms themselves, there are large distinctions based on social, economic, ethnic and educational factors.[40] Of course, some salutary effects accrue from this diversification. Perhaps it contributes to meeting more satisfactorily the diverse needs of our heterogeneous society. But on the whole, the gulfs which separate members of our profession give rise to many problems. The rash of current studies which point out these problems are helping us understand them better, and ameliorating efforts are being made on several fronts. How far the situation is changing is hard to tell, however. Perhaps it can only be satisfactorily known some twenty years from now.

Availability of the Profession

One significant result of the way the profession in the United States has developed was lamented in the 1930's in these terms: " The draining off of best brains into a single channel has meant that the fitting of law to new conditions has been concentrated on *only one phase* of new conditions: to wit, the furtherance of the business and financing side, *from the angle of the enterpriser and the financier.*"[41] The channelling of legal talent into the cause of big business is much less a problem today; instead a subtler, and probably

---

[40] Smigel, *The Wall Street Lawyer—Professional Organization Man?* 171–202 (1964).

[41] Llewellyn, " The Bar Specializes—With What Results?" 167 *Annals* 177, 179 (1933).

more serious, problem of the proper distribution of legal service faces the American bar. It has been observed that the
rapidly expanding, relatively affluent middle classes " with an
increasing need for legal services do not obtain in propor-
tionate measure the legal services they need, at least from
lawyers." [42] There is, in other words, a huge gap between
the need for legal assistance, particularly in the planning
stages, and its satisfaction by the profession. Several reasons
for this gap may be found. On the part of many laymen
there is ignorance of the need for and value of legal services
and fear of overcharging and overreaching by the lawyer.
On the lawyer's part, there is the restraint of the canons
barring advertising, representation of conflicting interests, and
lay intermediaries.

Already a number of cures have been experimented with.
For example, there is a lawyer referral service operated by the
local bar association in most cities. Typically, a panel of
lawyers agree to make their services available, and each takes
his turn in the referral office conducting the critical inter-
views with clients. There is a low fixed fee for the initial
consultation, and an understanding as to future fees is reached
with the client before further work is undertaken. To pro-
mote greater utilization of the service, suitable publicity is
often given through the local bar association.

Another means of providing broader legal assistance is the
unique Neighborhood Law Office Plan in Philadelphia. The
offices, set up in selected moderate-income areas are wholly
independent of one another. Limitations on fees and general
supervision are provided by the Philadelphia Bar Association,
and the 28 Neighborhood Law Offices serve 4,000 clients

[42] Cheatham, *A Lawyer When Needed* 60 (1963).

annually. Such efforts as these, made by the bar associations throughout the country, to bring important legal services to the great number of persons who have been going without them serve a very useful function. But in meeting broader public needs, great care will have to be taken to avoid sacrificing high ethical standards. As Judge Traynor of the California Supreme Court has said:

> "Given the primary duty of the legal profession to serve the public, the rules it establishes to govern its professional ethics must be directed at the performance of that duty. Canons of ethics that would operate to deny . . . [individuals] the effective legal assistance they need can be justified only if such a denial is necessary to suppress professional conduct that in other cases would be injurious to the effective discharge of the profession's duties to the public." [43]

Conclusion

Perhaps I have shown what a complex organism the bar of the United States is, both because of its size and diversity, and because of its history. As with almost everything in the United States, the wonder is, I think, that we do as well as we do. The obstacles which we have set up for ourselves are almost insuperable. Yet we keep trying, and we make progress, I think. If we do, this is due to the devoted efforts of hundreds of able and dedicated lawyers, now and in the past. For, in this welter of size and confusion, we have always been blessed with a surprising number of strong and able men, who are willing to devote their time, their energy and their abilities to the public good, and the good of their profession. Being a lawyer in the United States is sometimes trying to

---

[43] *Hilderbrand*-v. *State Bar*, 36 Cal. 2d 504, 522, 225 P. 2d 508, 519 (1950) (dissenting opinion).

the soul. But it has elements of inspiration. Without a long tradition, with a scattered and complicated history, and against great odds, we make our legal system work. We understand it ourselves, and seek to make it better. We can only hope that our friends will be tolerant of us in the light of the difficulties which we face.

CHAPTER 3

LEGAL EDUCATION IN THE UNITED STATES

A FURTHER dimension may be added to the picture of the legal profession in the United States which we have already seen, namely, the nature of the educational system in which the profession is trained. Legal education in the United States has had a different development from that in the United Kingdom, yet it is clearly traceable to an English origin. As Professor James Bradley Thayer wrote:

> "We transplanted an English root, and nurtured and developed it, while at home it was suffered to languish and die down. It was the great experiment in the University teaching of our law at Oxford, in the third quarter of the eighteenth century, and the publication, a little before the American Revolution, of the results of that experiment, which furnished the stimulus and the exemplar for our own early attempts at systematic legal education." [1]

APPRENTICESHIP

We have already seen that by the middle of the eighteenth century a considerable amount of apprentice education for young lawyers had developed in America. This was in accordance with the English pattern as it had grown up after

---

[1] Thayer, "The Teaching of English Law at Universities," 9 *Harv.L.Rev.* 169, 170 (1895).

the Inns of Court had ceased, towards the end of the seventeenth century, to fulfill satisfactorily their function in legal education. But much American legal education continued to consist of merely "reading law." Alexander Hamilton read law for three months under the guidance of Robert Troup. In July, 1782, he was admitted to practice as an attorney, and three months later, in October, 1782, he was admitted as a counselor.[2] There was no systematic instruction available in New York at that time, but the beginnings of American legal education were discernible in Virginia.

University Professorships

Under the Vinerian Professorship, Blackstone gave his lectures in a University. It should not be forgotten that he encountered opposition from the academic community, and that he felt that he had to justify his intrusion into an academic scene in the opening lecture. In the first section of the Introduction, entitled "On the Study of the Law," he referred to the "monastic prejudice" which he had to overcome.[3] Law has remained in English Universities, but as an academic subject. There has been little effort to professionalize English academic legal education, and any development in this direction is looked upon with disdain. Partly because of this, the gap between English legal academics and the practicing legal profession has remained wide. To a considerable extent they live and move in different worlds and have little professional contact.

In America, there were efforts to establish professorships

---

[2] Schachner, *Alexander Hamilton* 145–146 (1946).
[3] 1 Bl.Comm. *26.

of law in the 1770's, the first of which came to nought.[4]
But in 1779, Thomas Jefferson came into the picture, and we
find the following recorded in his autobiography:

> "On the 1st of June, 1779, I was appointed Governor of
> the Commonwealth, and retired from the legislature. Being
> elected, also, one of the Visitors of William and Mary college,
> a self-electing body, I effected, during my residence in
> Williamsburg that year, a change in the organization of that
> institution, by abolishing the Grammar school, and the two
> professorships of Divinity and Oriental languages, and sub-
> stituting a professorship of Law and Police, one of Anatomy,
> Medicine and Chemistry, and one of Modern languages. . . ."[5]

Jefferson's law tutor, George Wythe, was immediately
installed as the first professor. Wythe had been Attorney
General of Virginia at the age of 28, and he had been one of
the signers of the Declaration of Independence. He imme-
diately started on a distinguished career as a law teacher,
which lasted until his resignation ten years later, in 1789.
Among Wythe's outstanding pupils (some of them before
his appointment to the professorship) were John Marshall,
Spencer Roane, John Breckenridge, James Monroe, Henry
Clay, and Edmond Randolph. Wythe's course was based on
Blackstone as a textbook, and lectures comparing English and
Virginia law.[6]

When Wythe resigned, he was succeeded by another of
his students, St. George Tucker. Tucker likewise used

---

[4] A professorship was proposed by Governor Tryon at King's College, now
Columbia University, in 1774. Reed, *Training for the Public Profession
of the Law* 114 (1921). And in 1777 President Stiles of Yale proposed a
professorship of law. Holdsworth, *History of English Law*, vol. 12, 100
(1938).   [5] Jefferson, *Autobiography* 63 (Malone ed. 1959).
[6] See Devitt, " William and Mary: America's First Law School," 2 *Wm.
& Mary L.Rev.* 424 (1960). Wythe had about 40 students in 1780. In
1839 the William and Mary Law School had 30 students. Reed, *Training
for the Public Profession of the Law* 116 (1921).

Blackstone as his text, but he supplemented it with extensive notes designed to make it applicable to American outlook and conditions. Tucker's Blackstone, combining the original with these notes, was published in 1803, and was the leading law textbook in America for many years.

Though Wythe and Tucker were professors in a University, without being set up as a separate "law school," the difference is simply one of definition. There can be no doubt that Wythe and Tucker and their successors at William and Mary were engaged in a substantial, successful and influential venture in legal education, and that their effort can fairly be called the first law school in America. Unfortunately, the Civil War brought legal education at William and Mary to a stop in 1861. It was resumed in 1920, but the gap of nearly 60 years keeps it from being the oldest law school now in continuous operation in the United States.

In the last decade of the eighteenth century, similar lectureships were started elsewhere, but for the most part they did not last beyond a year or two. In 1790, James Wilson was appointed Professor of Law at the College of Philadelphia, now the University of Pennsylvania.[7] Wilson was a Justice of the Supreme Court of the United States, which at that time sat in Philadelphia, then the capital of the country. Though the lectures were laid out on a three year basis, Wilson withdrew at the end of the first year. In 1793, James Kent was appointed a Professor of Law at Columbia. After a few years, however, he resigned to take up his place on the bench, where he became one of the first great American judges. He resumed the lectures for a year in

[7] Hurst, *The Growth of American Law: The Law Makers* 258 (1950); Reed, *Training for the Public Profession of the Law* 122 (1921).

1824, and out of this came Kent's *Commentaries on American Law*, a work in the Blackstone manner, but essentially American in content and outlook. Though Kent's work did not displace Blackstone, it assumed a place beside the older work, and was of great influence in American legal education for many years.

Finally, reference should be made to a professorship of law which was established at Transylvania College, in Lexington, Kentucky, in 1799. George Nicholas, a graduate of William and Mary, was appointed the "Professor of Law and Politics." Later on, Henry Clay was for two years the incumbent of this professorship.[8] This was for two generations the only effort in legal education away from the eastern seabord.

LITCHFIELD LAW SCHOOL

Another type of development, of great significance to legal education was occurring at the same time, unconnected with any University. This was the Litchfield Law School, located, as Dean Ames has said, "On a broad shaded street in one of the most beautiful of New England villages."[9] Judge Tapping Reeve, a graduate of the College of New Jersey (now Princeton University) in 1772, at the head of his class, had gone into practice in Litchfield, Connecticut. Two years later, in 1774, he had as a pupil his brother-in-law, Aaron Burr. From time to time after that, other young men came to him as students. It is hard to fix an exact year when this

[8] Reed, *Training for the Public Profession of the Law* 118 (1921); Ames, "The Vocation of the Law Professor" (1901), in Ames, *Lectures on Legal History* 354, 359 (1913).

[9] Ames, *supra*, note 8, at 354.

process developed into a " school," but 1784 is generally taken as the opening date, for that is the year in which Reeve erected a one-story wooden building close to his house for the use of his students. In 1798 he took on one of his students, James Gould, a Yale graduate, as a partner. For many years, there were from 9 to 30 students. The peak year was reached in 1813, when there were 55 students. Instruction was through lectures lasting an hour and a half each day. There were regular examinations, and moot courts were conducted. The course lasted over a period of fourteen months.

The school closed in 1833, after an existence of nearly fifty years.[10] During that time it had something over a thousand students. Their names have been gathered together and published.[11] They include John C. Calhoun of South Carolina, Horace Mann of Massachusetts, and Levi Woodbury of New Hampshire, and Augustus Hand, the grandfather of the cousins Judges Learned and Augustus N. Hand. Twenty-eight of them became United States Senators, 101 members of Congress, 34 State Supreme Court justices, 14 governors of States and 10 lieutenant governors, 3 vice presidents of the United States, 3 United States Supreme Court Justices, and 6 members of the Cabinet. As Professor Joel Parker of the Harvard Law School said: " Perhaps no Law School has had—perhaps I may add ever will have—so great a proportion of distinguished men on its catalogue. . . ."[12]

---

[10] See Harno, *Legal Education in the United States* 28–34 (1953); Reed, *Training for the Public Profession of the Law* 128–132 (1921).

[11] Yale Law Library Publications, *Litchfield Law School* (1946).

[12] Parker, *The Law School of Harvard College* 8 (1871), quoted by Brown, *Lawyers and the Promotion of Justice* 27 (1938).

Harvard Law School

As an illustration of the development of the schools in which American lawyers are taught at the present time, let us look at the history of the Harvard Law School. The example is an appropriate one in view of the fact that this School has been widely used as a model by other schools, and that it has had some part in the legal education of 25% of all the law teachers in the United States.

For the beginning, we must turn the story back to 1781. In that year there died, in England, Isaac Royall, who, in a practical sense, is the founder of the Harvard Law School. Royall had been born in Massachusetts, and was a prosperous merchant of Medford, Massachusetts, where his mansion house is still preserved as a museum. He was a loyalist in the Revolution, and fled the country when hostilities came. He made his will in 1779, and died in 1781, leaving real estate in America to Harvard College for the purpose of establishing " a professorship of law or of physic." Because of the war and postwar situation, it was hard to realize on the land, and no action was taken until 1815. By that time the principal of the Royall Fund was somewhat under $10,000, and the annual income available for the professor was about $400. In 1815, Harvard established the Royall Professorship as a professorship of law, and Isaac Parker, the Chief Justice of the Supreme Judicial Court of Massachusetts, was named as the first professor. This was a professorship in Harvard College, and the function of the professor was to give lectures on law as a part of the regular undergraduate curriculum. The professor was also allowed to admit other persons, not members of the University, to his lectures, on such terms as he might choose, as long as he did not fail to make his lectures available to undergraduates.

In his inaugural address, Parker outlined the need for a separate law school, on a professional basis.[13] In Parker's view, this was to be a graduate school, thus following the pattern of the Divinity School at Harvard, rather than the Medical School.

Only two years later, Parker's recommendation was adopted by the Harvard Corporation (The President and Fellows of Harvard College, chartered by the Massachusetts Bay Colony in 1650, and the oldest corporation still extant in the United States). Thus, in 1817 the Harvard Law School was established. Asahel Stearns, a Congressman who had just lost his seat in the demise of the Federalist Party, was named a Professor in the Law School. He was called a University Professor of Law, but he was to be paid only out of the fees of students. These were fixed at $100 a year, that being the current rate for law office study at the time. Stearns continued to hold the office of County Attorney, and that was his principal source of income. The University's commitment was to provide two rooms, and $500 for the purchase of books for the library. The Law School started with one student, and the number entering during the first year was six.[14] Parker remained the Royall Professor, lecturing to College students. The Law School course was frankly professional, being based on Blackstone, and other common-law texts, supplemented by lectures dealing with American decisions, a moot court and debating clubs. Law students could attend the public lectures of the College, and were

[13] Warren, *History of the Harvard Law School*, vol. 1, 299–302 (1908).
[14] *Ibid.*, vol. 1, 333 (1908).

required to write a dissertation " upon some title or branch of the law or the history of some department of legal or political science." These were the only breaks in the purely professional nature of the Law School work. It seems obvious that the Law School was established to meet the competition provided by law office instruction, and particularly that provided by the Litchfield Law School, to which Chief Justice Parker had made reference in his opening address.[15]

Despite the fact that Parker had contemplated a graduate school, competition apparently was the cause of rapid lowering of standards. By 1825, it was announced that any person who was qualified to become a student of law in his home state might be received in the Law School.[16] Degrees (the LL.B.) were awarded to students who stayed for eighteen months, and met minimal requirements.[17] Of this early period in the history of the Harvard Law School, it has been said : " . . . it is only fair to recall that it was Harvard that gave the signal for encouraging a merely nominal connection between the college and the bar. She lent the prestige of her name to the doctrine that calling a practitioner a university professor is equivalent to making his proprietary law class a university law school; and that an academic law degree may properly be conferred upon students entirely destitute of academic training." [18]

But as so often happens, the lowering of standards did not lead to success or prosperity. As Dean Ames has said, " For

15 See Reed, *Training for the Public Profession of the Law* 137–140 (1921).
16 Currie, " The Materials of Law Study," 3 *J.Leg.Ed.* 331, 360 (1951).
17 The first LL.B. degrees were awarded to six men in 1820. See Warren, *History of the Harvard Law School*, vol. 1, 338–340 (1908).
18 Reed, *Training for the Public Profession of the Law* 140 (1921).

the first dozen years of its existence, the Harvard Law School was a languishing local institution." [19] By the fall of 1828–29 there were four students, and in the spring of 1829, there was only one. Parker's resignation as Royall Professor was requested and obtained in 1827. And in 1829, Stearns resigned in despair.[20] This was surely the low point for any school—no professors, and virtually no students.

Joseph Story

But there were those who were much interested in improving legal education, and the bright dawn was just ahead. In 1829, an event occurred which has its close parallel in Viner's establishment of the Vinerian Professorship. In that year, Nathan Dane, a distinguished American lawyer, draftsman of the Ordinance of 1787, which established the Northwest Territory, and the author of Dane's *General Abridgement and Digest of American Law*, was persuaded to devote some of his profits from the latter work to the reorganization of the Harvard Law School. He gave $10,000 (later increased to $15,000) to the Harvard Corporation for a Professorship which would bear his name, and also for a new building for the Law School, to be known as Dane Hall. (Indeed, for the next fifty years the School was generally known as the Dane Law School.) In making his gift, he suggested that Joseph Story should be named the Dane Professor. Story was then a Justice of the Supreme Court of the United States. He had come originally from nearby Salem, Massachusetts, and had recently become a member of

---

[19] Ames, " The Vocation of the Law Professor " (1901), in *Lectures on Legal History* 354, 359 (1913).
[20] Currie, " The Materials of Law Study," 3 *J.Leg.Ed.* 331, 360 (1951).

the Harvard Corporation, so the negotiations were apparently not difficult. Story accepted the appointment, but stipulated that another professor be named to handle all administrative matters. On June 3, 1829, Story was elected the Dane Professor, and held that post until his death in 1845.[21]

Story has himself given us the reasons for his undertaking these duties, while he continued to serve as a Justice of the Supreme Court of the United States. In a letter which he wrote to the Principal of the Dublin Law Institute,[22] he said:

> " I have long been persuaded that a more scientific system of legal education, than that which has hitherto been pursued, is demanded by the wants of the age and the progress of jurisprudence. The old mode of solitary, unassisted studies in the Inns of Court, or in the dry and uninviting drudgery of an office, is utterly inadequate to lay a just foundation for accurate knowledge in the learning of the law. It is for the most part a waste of time and effort, at once discouraging and repulsive. It was, however, the system in which I was myself bred; and so thoroughly convinced was I of its worthlessness, that I then resolved, if ever I had students, I would pursue an opposite course. It was my earnest desire to assist in the establishment of another system, which induced me to accept my present professorship in Harvard University, thereby burthening myself with duties and labors, which otherwise I would gladly have declined."

Story's school was an immediate success, and during his tenure, the patterns of American legal education were firmly set for a long time to come. His stature and ability were such that students soon began coming to the Harvard Law School from all parts of the country, and thus its character as

---

[21] See, generally, Warren, *History of the Harvard Law School*, vol. 1, 415–424 (1908).
[22] *9 Law Reporter* 142 (1846).

a National law school was soon established. In the first year of Story's tenure, 1829–30, there were 24 students. Ten years later there were 86. In 1841, there were 115 students, and in the fall of 1844, the last year of Story's career, there were 163.[23]

Story's school was a purely professional school. From the beginning of his appointment, it was provided that " No previous examination is necessary for admission to the School." Nevertheless, a considerable proportion of the students were college graduates. This ran from two-thirds to three-quarters in most of the years. In 1844, however, only 56% were college graduates, and this proportion declined still further in the years following Story's death.[24]

But Story's influence was clearly against any particular relation between legal education and general university studies, either as a prerequisite for law study, or as a part of that study. As one acute commentator has said, " the results were that for the next fifty years the necessity of university education as preparation for law study was to be denied, and the scope of the university law curriculum was given a narrowly professional definition which was to be controlling for more than a century." [25]

After Story's death, the Harvard Law School fell into the doldrums. It utilized the momentum which Story had given it, and it remained a National law school. But such standards as it inevitably had under a man like Story, and his co-professor Simon Greenleaf, slowly drifted away. By the 1860's, the School not only had no entrance requirements,

---

23 Reed, *Training for the Public Profession of the Law* 143, 450 (1921).
24 *Ibid.* 145–146 (1921).
25 Currie, " The Materials of Law Study," 3 *J.Leg.Ed.* 331, 361 (1951).

but it had no examinations for students, and no requirements for the law degree other than bare attendance for a minimal period of time. Again I quote from Dean Ames, who came to the School as a student, and then as a Faculty member, shortly after this period. He referred to it as "a school without examination for admission or for the degree." And he added that it had "a faculty of three professors giving but ten lectures a week to one hundred and fifteen students of whom fifty-three per cent. had no college degree, a curriculum without any rational sequence of subjects, and an inadequate and decaying library." [26]

A storm was building up. In 1869, a "rather derogatory report" was made to the Board of Overseers of Harvard College, by the Committee to Visit the Law School.[27] In 1870, an editorial (or leader) in the *American Law Review*, probably written by a recent graduate of the School, Oliver Wendell Holmes, Jr., said that "for a long time the condition of the Harvard Law School has been almost a disgrace to the Commonwealth of Massachusetts." [28] The gravamen of the complaint was found in the assertion that "a school which undertook to confer degrees without any preliminary

[26] Ames, "Christopher Columbus Langdell" (1909), in Ames, *Lectures on Legal History* 467, 477 (1913).

[27] See Warren, *History of the Harvard Law School*, vol. 2, 359 (1908).

[28] 5 *Am.L.Rev.* 177 (1870). The editorial note is unsigned, but at that time the editors of the *American Law Review* were Oliver Wendell Holmes, Jr., and Arthur G. Sedgwick. Holmes had been a student at the Harvard Law School in 1864–66, and Sedgwick in 1865–67. Judge Joel Parker, who had been the Royall Professor of Law until 1868 wrote a pamphlet in his own defence in which he referred to them as "two young men, it is understood, who about four years since, consented to receive the honors of the School in the shape of a degree of Bachelor of Laws." Parker, *The Law School of Harvard College* 5 (1871).

examination whatever was doing something every year to injure the profession throughout the country, and to discourage real students."

It is interesting to observe that the same complaint had been made about English legal education at a slightly earlier time. A recent author, referring to the Report of the Commissioners on the Study of the Law and Jurisprudence, made in 1855, has recounted: [29]

> " Several witnesses, including the Treasurer of Lincoln's Inn, doubted
>> ' the expediency of an Examination for the Call to the Bar, conceiving that . . . it would also deter country gentlemen and others who wished to be called to the Bar, with a view merely to acquire such status and so much professional knowledge as would be useful to them as Magistrates, Politicians, Legislators, and Statesmen; and this effect in the opinion of these witnesses would be a serious evil.'
>
> Although the Commissioners agreed that such a consequence would be regrettable, they pressed nonetheless for the institution of examinations."

That low standards were not confined to legal education at this time is shown by a rather remarkable and revealing statement, for which I am indebted to my colleague Professor Austin Wakeman Scott. This was made by Andrew Preston Peabody, Plummer Professor of Christian Morals, and Acting President of Harvard College, who, in his Report to the Board of Overseers of Harvard College for 1869, wrote as follows:

---

[29] Lucas, " Blackstone and the Reform of the Legal Profession," 77 *English Historical Review* 456, 480 (1962).

" There is, however, another growing tendency which is to be deprecated,—that of making a student's continued membership of College contingent mainly on his annual examinations. In the judgment of the undersigned, every student who maintains a blameless moral character, attends College exercises regularly, and is not culpably negligent in the preparation of his lessons from day to day, should be permitted to remain undisgraced and unmolested. There are many cases in which there coexists with an average capacity of liberal culture an irremediable deficiency as to the memory of words and details. We have had among our students of this description many persons of high respectability,—some of surpassing excellence. Such young men, by being suffered to complete their collegiate course without disgrace or drawback, are rendered ever after the loyal friends and often the generous benefactors of our higher educational institutions, and not unfrequently reflect honor on the Alma Mater on whose indulgence they drew so largely in their youth.

" The undersigned believes that it is of positive benefit to a college class to have a certain proportion of members of the kind under discussion. Their defect of memory will always keep them near the foot of the class; and by occupying that position they sustain the self-respect and ambition of those next above them. The ninetieth scholar in a class of a hundred has an appreciable rank, which he will endeavor at least to maintain, if possible to improve. But if the ten below him be dismissed or degraded, so that he finds himself at the foot of his class, the depressing influence of this position will almost inevitably check his industry and quench his ambition, so that he will sink to the lower grade on which the hundredth scholar stood. This process, if repeated, might bring the eightieth scholar down to the same level, and so on indefinitely."

During this period, the number of other schools slowly increased. By 1870, there were, in all, 31 law schools in the country. But their standards were equally low. Twelve of them had only a one year course, while the other 19 had courses of one and a half or two years.

Dean Langdell

In 1870, after the dark period, came a new dawn. In 1869 Charles William Eliot, a chemist, became the President of Harvard University, and he immediately set out to re-organize the Law School and the Medical School of the University. In January, 1870, he brought to the Law School a bookish New York lawyer named Christopher Columbus Langdell, as Dane Professor of Law, and in September, 1870, Langdell was made the Dean of the Law School, a title which had not previously been used.

Under Langdell, numerous changes were introduced, all of which have had great impact on legal education in the United States. He quickly brought in a strong young faculty. He invented and introduced the case method of instruction. In 1878 the passing of three annual examinations was made a requisite for the law degree. But it was difficult to increase entrance requirements. For many years all that was required for admission to the Harvard Law School was the passage of examinations in a foreign language, English and Blackstone. It was not until 1894 that Harvard announced that beginning in 1896 it would admit only persons who had a degree from an approved college, or were eligible for admission to the senior year at Harvard College. The latter alternative was dropped a few years later, and for nearly seventy years now Harvard has required a college degree for admission, and the passing of annual examinations in three years for graduation. Despite early weaknesses and shortcomings, Harvard was a pacemaker in establishing these educational requirements.

Much has been written about the case method of instruction. It was long a battleground in the United States, but that is long since past. The case method has won on all fronts, though it has been modified and developed to meet new conditions. Langdell was much influenced by the growing scientific spirit of his time. He thought of the library as the laboratory of the law student, and the cases were the molecules and atoms which needed to be analyzed and fitted together. Putting the cases into casebooks was partly a matter of convenience for the students, and partly a practical matter of protecting the library so that the books there would not wear out. But it was far more than that. It was a method for showing the development of doctrine, and for leading students to ascertain for themselves the essential principles of the law and modes of analysis used by the judges. On this basis he produced his *Selection of Cases on the Law of Contracts*, published in 1871. Since that time hundreds of casebooks have followed, and the making of casebooks has been perhaps the principal preoccupation of law professors. The case method of teaching has been subject to continuous criticism,[30] but in its various forms—the concrete,

---

[30] These are summarized in Harno, *Legal Education in the United States* 137–140 (1953). See also Patterson, "The Case Method in American Legal Education: Its Origins and Objectives," 4 *J.Leg.Ed.* 1 (1951); Morgan, "The Case Method," 4 *J.Leg.Ed.* 379 (1952).

The earliest, and perhaps the most trenchant criticism of the case method was written by O. W. Holmes, Jr., in reviewing the second edition of Dean Langdell's casebook. He wrote: "Mr. Langdell's ideal in the law, the end of all his striving, is the *elegantia juris*, or *logical* integrity of the system as a system. He is, perhaps, the greatest living legal theologian. But as a theologian, he is less concerned with his postulates than to show that the conclusions from them hang together." 14 *Am.L.Rev.* 233 (1880).

specific, or problem method—it remains the predominant method of legal instruction in the United States today.

Law Reviews

One important development came in the next decade. This was the founding of the *Harvard Law Review* in 1887, two years after the *Law Quarterly Review* was begun. The peculiarly American, and remarkable thing about this journal, which has had great influence on legal education in the United States, is that the *Review* was founded by students, and has always been operated by a student board, on their own responsibility. They are free to consult the Faculty as much as they wish, but they make their own decisions. Moreover, a considerable portion of the material printed, including comments and criticisms of current court decisions and legislative enactments, is written by students.

The editorial board of the *Harvard Law Review* numbers about 58 students, 25 in the second year class, and 33 in the third year class, chosen on the basis of their standing in the Law School examinations. In the early days, the *Law Review* had some of the elements of a private club, and it chose its members somewhat arbitrarily. But since the First World War, the rule has been established that the selection must be made strictly from the rank list in the annual examinations, omitting no one who ranks above a selected cut-off point on the list.

The *Law Review* provides some very useful legal commentary. It tends to be too tightly written for easy reading, and to bury itself in footnotes designed to show that the students have been diligent and have not overlooked any possibly relevant materials. But the achievement is a remarkable one, that in a learned profession the basic periodical commentaries are written and edited by students. And the legal education provided for the members of the Board is remarkably good. The editors put in very long hours, and they tend to neglect their regular classwork. But in their writing, rewriting, editing, discussing, even in their proofreading and citation checking, they learn a great deal of law, and a great deal about law.

The example of the *Harvard Law Review* has led to a great proliferation of Law Reviews in the United States. Yale and Columbia followed soon; and now the situation is that virtually every law school must have a law review. There are at least ninety of these law reviews altogether. Of course this adds to the welter of words in which our law is buried, and increases problems not only for law schools, law libraries and law teachers, but also for practitioners. A considerable amount of material printed in law reviews is not worth printing. But much is good, and some very good. Consequently, one must use the indexes, and pick and choose. With a little care and effort, he has the advantage of examining some careful thought on almost any legal question.

Incidentally, one good and rather remarkable thing about American legal practitioners is the fact that within very wide limits, they are generous in sharing their experiences and skills with other lawyers. American law offices do not ordinarily regard their solutions to problems as " trade secrets " which they must jealously guard as a means of maintaining their preeminence. Many of our best practitioners record the fruits of their labors and experience in carefully prepared articles in the law reviews, and these are helpful not only to other lawyers but also to the courts. And the practitioners frequently participate in " Institutes " and other programs

which are a part of " Continuing Legal Education " for the
benefit of younger lawyers and practitioners generally. In
this way, there is a considerable amount of professional feeling and camaraderie among the bar which helps to make up
for our lack of close-knit professional organizations such as
the Inns of Court, or the Law Society.

Present Day Standards

By the turn of the century, the pattern of American legal
education was finally set. Subsequent developments have
been along the lines finally laid out by Langdell and his
associates.

In 1893 the American Bar Association established a Section
on Legal Education. The Section pressed for the extension
of the law course to three years. It also recommended an
organization for the law schools, and, as a result, The Association of American Law Schools came into being in 1900.
Its first President was James Bradley Thayer, of the Harvard
Law School. The Association remained under the wing of
the American Bar Association until 1913, holding its meetings
at the same time and place as the Bar Association. But in
1914 it broke away, and it has met separately ever since.
Nevertheless relations between the two Associations have
remained close and generally harmonious.

The Bar Association has continued to have a Section on
Legal Education and Admission to the Bar. In 1920, Elihu
Root was elected Chairman of the Section, and a special committee was established, with Root as Chairman, to report on
the steps which should be taken " to create conditions which
will tend to strengthen the character and improve the efficiency of persons to be admitted to the practice of law." This

Committee reported in 1922, and its recommendations were immediately approved by the Section and by the American Bar Association. The report laid down minimum standards for law schools, which included a minimum of two years of college as a prerequisite for admission to law school, and a law school course of at least three years, and longer where law was studied on a part-time basis. The report further provided that schools should be inspected, and that a list should be made up of those which were approved as meeting the standards of the American Bar Association. There was strong opposition to these developments at the time, but this opposition has died out with the passage of the years.

The Council of the Section on Legal Education and Admission to the Bar proceeded with the task of inspecting schools. In 1923 it published a list of 39 schools which complied with the standards, and a second list of 9 additional schools which had taken steps to bring themselves into compliance. The Section has a paid Adviser who supervises the inspection of the schools—which are reinspected from time to time. In 1950, the Bar Association, on recommendation of the Section, increased the requirement for pre-legal education to at least three years of college study, and the Association of American Law Schools adopted the same requirement. At the present time, there are 128 law schools which have been approved by the American Bar Association, and 108 schools which meet the slightly higher requirements for membership in the Association of American Law Schools.

Most of the States have adopted the standards of the American Bar Association in determining the qualification of persons who can be considered for admission to the bar. A number of States, and a considerable number of law schools, now have a requirement of a college degree before a student can be admitted to law study. Thus, in the schools with the highest requirements, a total period of study after high school or preparatory school, aggregating seven years is required, four years of general education in college, and three years of professional education in law school. As a result, our law students are usually from twenty-two to twenty-five years old, and the typical graduate is not able to start his work in practice until he has reached the age of twenty-five. This may be delayed from one to three years longer if the student has become involved in military service, or if he obtains some sort of foreign scholarship or fellowship.

At the present time there are about 54,000 students in American law schools.[31] Of these, around 50,000 are studying in schools approved by the American Bar Association. Of the total, about two-thirds are in three-year full-time schools, and one-third are in part-time schools, usually requiring four or five years of such work for the completion of the course. A total of about 10,000 young Americans are being admitted to the bar each year. This is about the same number of admissions as were being made thirty years ago, when the population of the country was only about two-thirds of what it is now. It does not seem likely, though, that the country is facing a lawyer shortage. The great increase in standards for admission to law school, and for graduation from law school, has resulted in a marked increase in the average caliber of those presenting themselves for admission to the bar. A generation ago, many of those being admitted were very poorly qualified, and were not in a position to make themselves very effective as lawyers. A far higher proportion of the present law school graduates are well qualified and

[31] ABA. Section of Legal Education and Admissions to the Bar, *Review of Legal Education* 19 (1963).

will make for themselves effective careers in the legal profession.

WHO ARE THE LAW STUDENTS?

In closing this discussion of legal education in the United States, let me make reference to some further material of a sociological nature, which is just beginning to become available as far as the legal profession is concerned. In the United States, the basic educational system is public and free. We have gone to great lengths to make basic educational opportunity available to all, regardless of family background or financial condition. In the process we have had to accept some losses in the quality of education provided, but we have thought that making it available in quantity was worth the price, and we have wrestled with the matter of quality.

As far as legal education and law practice are concerned, we likewise endeavor to eliminate barriers, and there are now no legal barriers based on race, religion or financial means to admission to law school or to law practice. But there are other factors which enter into the selection of those who actually become our lawyers and we are only now becoming aware of these in some detail.

Recently there has been a very preliminary study of students graduating from college (as we say) in 1961. This shows, as would be expected, that despite considerable equality in the availability of legal education, there is a good deal of self-selection in the process which determines those who will avail themselves of it. More than twice as many of those entering law school come from families whose household head is a professional person as of those who do not go to law school; and prospective lawyers are less likely to come from families where the household head is in a manual occupation. The same element of difference is encountered where family income is concerned. Thus it appears that prospective lawyers come disproportionately from one element of the population, and this may be thought of, in our setting, as the educated upper middle class.

In terms of religion, a higher proportion of Catholics and Jews than of Protestants choose to undertake law study. Proportionately more students from cities choose law than those from smaller places, but this may simply be a reflection of the family factors which have been referred to above.

In terms of academic ability, there is a high correlation with the choice of law as a career. The number of graduating seniors preferring law among the top 20% of the college students is twice the number preferring law among all male students. Similarly, prospective law students are more likely to have gone to private colleges which charge relatively high tuitions and attract students of superior academic quality.

As to the particular law school the students attend, academic achievement is clearly an important factor. Fifty-eight per cent of the top students academically entered 8 schools, with high academic standards, while these schools took only 21% of the medium students and 3% of those with low academic standings. The proportions were more nearly equal in the next group of 16 law schools. And the remaining 100 law schools had 28% of the top group of students, 41% of those in the middle, and 73% of the lowest group. Again there was close correlation with family income and father's education.[32] In addition, though there are no

[32] These and other data based on a study of over 1,000 graduates electing law study in June, 1961, are contained in Lawyers in the Making, Report No. 96 of the National Opinion Research Center, University of Chicago, December, 1963. The material will be further analyzed and published under the auspices of the American Bar Foundation.

rigid lines, and such lines as there are are slowly disappearing, a high proportion of the partners in the larger firms come from a small number of the law schools.[33] To a large degree, the lines we have previously considered, which divide the profession, begin to form even before the formal study of the law commences.

The significance of these law school figures is far from clear. They do not necessarily show that there is any sort of discrimination in admission to law study except such as results from differences in ability, with family background recognized as at least statistically relevant in determining academic abilities. They do show, however, that a relatively few law schools are entrusted with a high proportion of the nation's resources in ability. This puts on these schools a responsibility, shared, too, by all other schools, to utilize their resources in the most effective manner.

The studies into the social and cultural make-up of those who choose to study and practice law in America are still in a very rudimentary stage. No doubt future studies will bring to light more factors of the sort we have mentioned. Whatever the value of these studies and whatever the explanation for the data they reveal, one thing is clear. If high standards at the bar are to be developed and maintained, there must be high standards for entry into legal education and for admission to the bar. The road to that end has already been a long one, and we have made great progress. But there remain many problems to be resolved.

[33] See Carlin, *Lawyers on Their Own* 32 (1962).

CHAPTER 4

LEGAL QUESTIONS IN A FEDERAL SYSTEM

THE AREA OF DIVERSITY—STATE LAW

THE United States is a common law country, and its judges are common law judges. As is to be expected, there are certain basic similarities between the law practiced and administered there and the common law of England. Like you, we have torts, contracts, agency, evidence and all the other subjects which arise from the nature of human relationships. But there are also great dissimilarities, for we have fifty-one separate jurisdictions—the fifty States and the District of Columbia—each deciding common law questions for itself. Each has its own legislature, with power to enact statutes for its territory; and each has its own supreme court, with power to interpret the statutes and to decide nonstatutory questions in accordance with the customs and precedents of the particular jurisdiction and with the court's own good judgment. Thus, we have at least fifty-one versions of the common law in the United States, and it would be quite impossible for any person to be familiar with all of them.

As an illustration, we may take the question whether a pre-existing debt is consideration for a contract. That is an old question of the common law on which the law of England has long been clear. But in the United States, some courts have felt free to reconsider the matter, with the result that we have varying rules in different States.[1] Or take the matter

---

[1] See Williston, *Contracts*, Vol. 1, sec. 120 (3d ed. 1957).

of contributory negligence as a defense to tort liability. The common law rule was that contributory negligence was an absolute bar to any recovery by the plaintiff.[2] This rule is still followed in many of the United States.[3] But in some States—sometimes by statute and sometimes by judicial decision—we have the rule of comparative negligence,[4] similar to that followed in admiralty. In others we have extensive development of the rule of "last clear chance"; and in one state, Missouri, the courts have developed what is known as the "humanitarian doctrine,"[5] under which the owner of a particularly dangerous instrumentality, such as a train, will be held liable if he might have avoided the injury by the use of reasonable care, notwithstanding the plaintiff's contributory negligence.

I could go on with many other illustrations in the common law area. There is scarcely any rule which is uniformly followed in the United States. Sometimes there is a rule which is the law in a great majority of the States; but almost always there are one or more States, which, for one reason or another, have developed a different view. And on many questions there may be three or more rules, each followed by a considerable number of States. I think you can see that this makes law teaching in the United States rather interesting, as well as complicated, especially when the teaching is done in a school which draws its students from every part of the country. Among other things, it provides what I have called " a built in comparative law " approach. Law teaching does not consist in disseminating rules of law. Rather the

---

[2] See *Butterfield* v. *Forrester* (1809) 11 East 60.

[3] *E.g.*, *Smith* v. *Ohio Oil Co.*, 10 Ill.App.2d 67, 134 N.E.2d 526 (1956).

[4] See, *e.g.*, *Chism* v. *Phelps*, 228 Ark. 936, 311 S.W.2d 297 (1958).

[5] See *Murphy* v. *Wabash R.R.*, 228 Mo. 56, 76 S.W. 706 (1910).

student is encouraged to consider which one of the several views on any question is the "better" one, the more persuasive, the most consistent with the law as a whole, or the one most likely to meet the test of social utility. He is taught to question, to analyze, to compare, to consider, rather than to memorize. It is hardly surprising that much of this approach remains with him when he goes into practice, and even if, in due course, he should go onto the bench.

Quite apart from this checkerboard nature of our law, we have other problems which do not occur in your system. All of our courts operate under a written constitution. Indeed in each of the fifty States there are two constitutions which are applicable—the Federal Constitution, and the constitution of that State. Only in the District of Columbia is there a single constitution, for there the Constitution of the United States alone is in force. Not only do our courts operate under these written constitutions, but they proceed in the context of the Federal system which is established by these constitutions. Most ordinary questions, like those of torts and contracts, are questions of State law, where each State is free to decide for itself, and neither the Federal Congress, nor the Federal Supreme Court have any authority at all.

There are also many Federal questions, that is, questions which arise under the Federal Constitution, or under statutes passed by Congress, or under treaties with other nations. And on these Federal questions, the Supreme Court of the United States has the final authority, and its decisions are binding on all of the State courts. So we have uniform Federal law on Federal questions, and diverse State law on State questions. Thus we have achieved a considerable measure of diversity in unity, and this may indeed be the mechanism which makes it possible for us to govern, after a fashion, so many people, with so many different backgrounds and traditions, over so vast and varied a territory. Still, though it is probably necessary, it is complicated. Only an American who has grown up in the system, and come to think of it as a part of the order of nature, can fail to see how intricate it is.

State Law and the Federal Courts

We have already seen that there are two complete sets of courts in the United States. In every State there are both State courts and Federal courts, with at least one United States district court in each State, a complete system of Federal courts of appeal and, at the top of the Federal judiciary, the United States Supreme Court. Does this mean that the common law in the United States, which, as we have seen, may vary widely from State to State, may also vary between the sets of courts within each State? This has been a very vexing question for our Federal system. To understand its answer, we must first understand something of the jurisdiction of the Federal courts.

Two major categories of cases make up most of the cases which the Federal courts have authority to hear. First, these courts may entertain cases arising under the Constitution, laws and treaties of the United States; we call these " Federal questions." They include crimes against the United States, such as violating the Federal income tax laws, stealing United States government property, or robbing the mails, or using the mails for illegal purposes. Robbery and embezzlement from nearly all American banks, which are insured by an agency of the Federal government, are likewise Federal offenses. Federal questions are also presented by civil suits under Federal statutes, such as the antitrust laws or the Fair Labor Standards Act, fixing hours of labor and minimum wages for business engaged in interstate commerce.

The second major group of Federal court cases arises under what is known as "diversity of citizenship" jurisdiction. Under this grant of jurisdiction and within limits set by Congress as to the amount in controversy, the Federal courts may hear any case, regardless of its subject-matter, where the plaintiff and defendant are citizens of different States or where one of the parties is a citizen of a foreign country. Diversity jurisdiction was established in part out of the fear that a State court might be biased against an out-of-State plaintiff, who might otherwise have no choice but to sue in such a forum. There was also some desire that the Federal government take a hand in assuring the steady dispensation of justice.[6]

Where diversity of citizenship and the requisite jurisdictional amount exist, a plaintiff may choose to bring his suit in either the State or the Federal courts. And in some cases, I should add, it is possible for a defendant who is sued in a State court to have the action removed to a Federal court. Thus, within certain limits, there will be a large number of cases which might be heard in one or the other of the two sets of courts which sit in each State.

Ideally, it should make no difference which court hears the case, but in fact the choice of court may be a very important matter. In the first place, the judges in the Federal courts are appointed by the President and hold their offices for life or during good behavior. In most of the States (but

---

[6] See Hart and Wechsler, *The Federal Courts and the Federal System* 24 (1953).

not all), the judges are elected and hold office for a term of years, sometimes a fairly short term. Traditionally, the judges in the Federal courts have wider powers with respect to juries. They may comment on the evidence, for example, though many of them do not exercise this power very freely. In many of the States, the judges can only summarize the evidence, but cannot express any view with respect to it.

These matters to one side, a major factor in choosing a State or Federal forum for litigation is the question of the law to be applied. If a Federal statute is in point, the question is relatively easy; that statute will be applied whether the case is heard in a State or a Federal court. If it is a matter of the common law, the State court will, of course, apply its own State law—including, in an appropriate case, its rules of conflict of laws, which may lead to the ultimate application of the law of another State. But what law will be applied in a Federal court?

The Early Rule

Historically, the great decision on this question was rendered in 1842 by the Supreme Court of the United States in the case of *Swift* v. *Tyson*.[7] In this case, Swift, a citizen of the State of Maine, sued Tyson, a citizen of New York, in the Federal court in New York City. Swift's suit was based on a bill of exchange which he held as endorsee, and which Tyson had accepted, and it was in the Federal court solely because of diversity of citizenship. There had been failure of consideration as to the bill of exchange, so Tyson had a defense unless Swift was a holder in due course. It was

[7] 16 Peters 1 (U.S. 1842).

agreed that Swift had taken before maturity, and without notice of any defect. The only question arose as to whether Swift had taken for value. It appeared that he had taken the bill of exchange in payment of a note he held and which had been made by the person who had endorsed the bill of exchange to him. Thus the question was directly presented whether discharge of the antecedent debt constituted value in connection with the endorsement of the bill.

The opinion in the case was written by Mr. Justice Story, who was then the senior Associate Justice of the United States Supreme Court, and a towering figure in American law. He reviewed the decisions of the New York courts on this question, and found them uncertain, though leaning in the direction of holding that discharge of a pre-existing debt is not consideration. At this point, Justice Story referred to section 34 of the Judiciary Act of 1789, one of the first statutes enacted by the Congress of the United States. This section provided (and still substantially provides today) that " the laws of the several states, except where the constitution, treaties or statutes of the United States shall otherwise require or provide, shall be regarded as rules of decision in trials at common law in the courts of the United States in cases where they apply."

Under this statute, the question was whether the decisions of the New York courts on the question at issue were " laws." Mr. Justice Story held that this statutory provision applied only to the statutes of the State " and the construction thereof adopted by the local tribunals, and to rights and titles to things having a permanent locality, such as rights and titles to real estate, and other matters immovable and intraterritorial

in their nature and character." [8]   As a result he held that
New York law was not controlling on the matter before the
Court. It was, he said, a matter governed by "the general
principles of commercial jurisprudence," [9] which the courts
of the United States were as well, or better, qualified to
determine as were the courts of New York. Regarding the
question as one of general law, he held that the pre-existing
debt was a valid consideration, and accordingly that Swift
should prevail, despite the fact that the courts of New York
would probably decide to the contrary.

The problem raised involves important jurisprudential
conceptions. What is the nature of the common law, or of
the "general law" as Justice Story referred to it? Is it the
command of a sovereign, in the Austinian sense, that is, something ordained by a governmental body? If so, the sovereign
here would presumably be the State of New York, since the
Federal Government has no power to make laws about such
matters. Or is the "common law" a more general conception, "a brooding omnipresence in the sky," in the phrase
later used by Justice Holmes? [10]   Is the common law to be
derived by reason, from general principles available to all
judges, or is it to be authoritatively determined by a State
having sovereign powers in the area?

Justice Story chose the "general law" approach for the
Federal Courts. This may have been partly due simply to a
conclusion on his part, shared by his colleagues on the
Supreme Court, that they were, on the whole, better qualified
to determine such questions than were the judges of the State

---

[8] *Id*. at 18.
[9] *Id*. at 19.
[10] *Southern Pac. Co.* v. *Jensen*, 244 U.S. 205, 222 (1917) (dissenting opinion).

courts. It was probably also the thought of the Justices who participated in the decision in *Swift* v. *Tyson* that the result they reached would be a strong influence towards unifying the law of the United States. Their decision on these questions would be binding in all of the Federal Courts throughout the country, and they no doubt hoped that the State courts would often defer to the Federal rule, with the result that the Federal rule would eventually become established in all courts, both State and Federal, throughout the country. As Mr. Justice Story said, quoting Cicero in Latin, "There will not be a law for Rome, or a law for Athens, a law for now, a law for then, but a single law will prevail among all nations and at all times."

The Early Rule in Practice

The rule of *Swift* v. *Tyson* lasted for nearly a century. It can at least be said that it received a fair trial. It was widely applied, in many fields of the law, in tort cases,[11] as well as in contract and commercial matters. But as an influence towards unification of the law it was thoroughly disappointing. The State courts did not choose to yield to the various rules of law established in the Federal courts. On the contrary, they regarded themselves as being as well qualified to decide questions of common or general law as were the Federal courts, and they went ahead and decided these questions according to their best judgment. Thus, we not only had varied State rules on numerous common law questions, but we also had a Federal rule on these questions, which

---

[11] *Baltimore & Ohio R.R.* v. *Baugh*, 149 U.S. 368 (1893).

might or might not be the same as the rule in the particular State where the Federal Court was sitting.

This was not only complicated, it was stultifying. Where a lawsuit was between two citizens of the same State, it would be heard in the State court, and decided according to the State rule. But if the same question arose in the same State, but with one of the parties a citizen of a different State, it might be heard in a Federal court, and decided according to the Federal rule of general law. And this rule might be different from the State rule, as was the case in *Swift* v. *Tyson*. Sometimes there might be two or more parties on one side of the same transaction, and one would win in one court while the other would lose in the other court. It was really a bizarre situation, but there seemed to be no escape from it. It appeared for many years to be an inherent consequence of our Federal system, with its dual and coordinate courts.

Of course the rule of *Swift* v. *Tyson* led to "forum shopping." A plaintiff would have to consider carefully both the law of the State and the "general law" applied in the Federal courts. One might be favorable and the other adverse, and he would select his forum accordingly, filing his suit in the State court if that law was favorable to him or in the Federal court if that law was favorable, and he could meet the jurisdictional requirements. This meant, too, that it was often impossible to plan any transaction safely. For it could not be settled in advance whether possible litigation would be heard in the State court, where one rule applied, or in a Federal court, where another rule might be applicable.

To make matters worse, Federal jurisdiction could sometimes be "manufactured." This was done in the famous case of *Black & White Taxicab Co.* v. *Brown & Yellow Taxicab Co.*[12] There a Kentucky railroad company had made a contract with a Kentucky taxi and transfer company giving the latter the exclusive privilege to go upon the railroad property and solicit taxi and transfer business. Such an exclusive arrangement was against the public policy of Kentucky. So, when another company sought to be admitted to equal privileges, the Kentucky taxi and transfer company was dissolved, with the cooperation of the railroad, and all of its rights, including its rights under the exclusive contract, were transferred to a newly organized Tennessee corporation. This Tennessee corporation then brought a suit in the Federal court in Kentucky against the competing company, claiming Federal jurisdiction on the basis of diversity of citizenship. It sought to have a Federal rule upholding such exclusive contracts applied, and it prevailed. Thus not only did the outcome of the litigation turn on the court in which it was brought, but the plaintiff corporation was created for the purpose of getting the case (which was in all essentials a local Kentucky case) into the Federal court and thus avoiding the Kentucky rule.

Justice Holmes dissented, joined by Justices Brandeis and Stone. His opinion was prophetic. In it he said that the rule of *Swift* v. *Tyson* was based upon a fallacy that there is such a thing as this " outside " general law, and that this " fallacy has resulted in an unconstitutional assumption of powers by the Courts of the United States which no lapse of time or respectable array of opinion should make us hesitate to correct." [13]

[12] 276 U.S. 518 (1928).
[13] *Id*. at 533.

The Modern Rule

It is perhaps one of the earmarks of the common law as it has developed in the United States—using the term " common law " in a broad sense to include the customs, traditions and methods of the courts—that our courts have always been freer in overruling their own decisions than has been the rule, at least recently, in England. Ours has been much more a trial-and-error approach. We recognize that courts may fall into error, and when a court is convinced that it has done so, we recognize it as not only its privilege but often its duty to correct that error. This is particularly true in the field of Constitutional law, where the error cannot be corrected by the legislature, and the process of Constitutional amendment is slow and difficult.

This was the background for the famous case of *Erie R.R.* v. *Tompkins*,[14] which was decided in 1938, ninety-six years after *Swift* v. *Tyson* had come down. Tompkins was walking along the tracks of the Erie Railroad in Pennsylvania and was injured by something projecting from an Erie train. He brought suit against the Erie in a Federal Court in New York, relying on diversity of citizenship as the basis for Federal jurisdiction. Under the law of Pennsylvania it was contended that Tompkins was a trespasser and that the Railroad would not be liable to him unless its negligence was willful or wanton. But the Federal district court and the intermediate United States Court of Appeals both held that the question was one of " general law," which should be decided by a Federal rule. Under this Federal rule, they held that recovery could be had for ordinary negligence. The Railroad then sought review by the United States Supreme

[14] 304 U.S. 64 (1938).

Court through a petition for a writ of certiorari, and this was granted.

When the case was heard, counsel for the Railroad urged that *Swift* v. *Tyson* was not applicable in this sort of case, but he did not question the validity or propriety of that decision; nor was any such question raised by the Court at the argument. But when the case was decided, *Swift* v. *Tyson* was overruled. In an opinion by Mr. Justice Brandeis, the Court held that the law of Pennsylvania was controlling. He held that *Swift* v. *Tyson* had not only been wrongly decided but that it was wrong as a matter of constitutional law. Under *Swift* v. *Tyson* the Federal courts had sought to develop decisional law in areas which under the Federal scheme were entrusted to the States, and in which the Congress was clearly without power to legislate. For the judicial branch of the Federal government to make law in these State-controlled areas was, according to Justice Brandeis, as much a usurpation as for the legislative branch to try to do the same. He went on to hold that where the Federal courts are given jurisdiction over non-federal causes of action, it is simply a jurisdiction to administer the laws of the States. He held that this conclusion was required as a constitutional matter, and not merely as a construction of section 34 of the Judiciary Act of 1789, to which reference has been made above.[15] The problem is clearly one arising out of our Federal system, and the solution reached by the Court through Mr. Justice Brandeis is based on the nature of that system.

The Applicable Conflict of Laws Rule

While the *Erie* decision resolved many of the problems created by *Swift* v. *Tyson*, it created many new and, perhaps,

[15] See p. 67, *supra*.

more complex problems. For example, what if the case in the Federal court involves a question of conflict of laws? Actually that was the situation in the *Erie* case. Mr. Justice Brandeis apparently assumed that if State law applied it would be the law of Pennsylvania, where the accident occurred, though the Federal trial court where the suit was brought sat in New York. In many cases, however, the conflict of laws rule is not so clear, and State and Federal notions of the proper rule may differ. Is conflict of laws to be treated as simply a part of the State law, or is it, because of its nature, to be the subject of a Federal rule which could be uniform in all Federal courts?

This question was soon presented to the Supreme Court in *Klaxon Co.* v. *Stentor Elec. Mfg. Co.*[16] The Court held that the Federal courts must regard conflict of laws as a part of the State law, and that they must apply the conflict of laws rules of the State in which they sit. This was thought to be simply a necessary consequence of the *Erie* rule, the underlying basis of which was that different results should not be reached in two courts sitting side by side, simply because of the accident of diversity of citizenship.

The *Klaxon* rule has been criticized as not required by the *Erie* case [17] and as encouraging geographical forum shopping among States in the name of discouraging forum shopping within a State. But since the States in a Federal system such as ours are undoubtedly free to adopt their own rules of substantive law, some amount of forum shopping is inevitable. A major purpose of having a Federal system is to allow for

[16] 313 U.S. 487 (1941).
[17] See Hart and Wechsler, *The Federal Courts and the Federal System* 633–636 (1953); Weintraub, "The Erie Doctrine and State Conflict of Law Rules," 39 *Ind.L.J.* 228 (1964).

some diversity, and where there is diversity there will be variations in result depending on where the suit is brought. It has been thought by some that a Federal doctrine of conflict of laws would help to achieve uniformity of results on particular sets of facts by requiring application of the one appropriate rule of law. If, in some way, the Federal courts could control the States in their selection of conflict of laws rules, we might indeed achieve a considerable measure of uniformity under the *Klaxon* doctrine. As yet, though, it has not been seriously contended that the ordinary choice of laws rules formulated in the several States are anything but ordinary rules of law which they are free to adopt as they see fit.

The Law Applicable in a " Transferred " Case

One other complication in our system of Federal courts applying State law has recently been dealt with by the United States Supreme Court, and should be referred to here. It sometimes happens that the Federal court in which an action is brought, or to which it has been removed, is a very inconvenient forum for the litigation, under all the circumstances. Many defendants, particularly corporate defendants, can be served with process in a number of States, some of which may be far from the place where the events in litigation occurred or from the place where many or most of the witnesses reside. To deal with this situation, Congress in 1948 enacted a provision allowing the " transfer " of suits from one Federal District Court to another. This is section 1404 (a) of the Judicial Code of 1948, and it reads as follows:

> " For the convenience of parties and witnesses, in the interest of justice, a district court may transfer any civil action to any other district or division where it might have been brought."

Early in 1964 the Supreme Court considered the case of *Van Dusen* v. *Barrack*,[18] which arose out of a disastrous crash of an Eastern Airlines plane in Boston Harbor in 1960. The flight was scheduled to operate from Boston, in Massachusetts, to Philadelphia, in Pennsylvania, and many of the passengers who were lost had their homes in one or the other of these cities. As a result of the accident, over 150 actions for personal injury and wrongful death were filed against the airline, various manufacturers of airplanes and airplane engines, the United States, and the Massachusetts Port Authority. More than 100 actions were brought in the United States District Court for Massachusetts, and more than 45 actions in the United States District Court for the Eastern District of Pennsylvania. The defendants in the Pennsylvania court moved that the cases there be transferred to Massachusetts under section 1404 (a), and whether this could or should be done was the question which came before the Supreme Court.

One of the problems presented arose out of the question as to what law would be applied if the cases were transferred. Many of the plaintiffs in Pennsylvania were executors or administrators appointed in that State, who might not have authority under Massachusetts law to maintain a suit in Massachusetts. Similarly, the Massachusetts statute of limitations might be shorter than that in Pennsylvania, with the result that some of the actions might be barred if the cases were transferred and Massachusetts law were held to apply, under the doctrine of the *Erie* case. Believing that a change in the applicable law would accompany the transfer, the United States Court of Appeals for the Third Circuit held

18 376 U.S. 612 (1964).

that it would not be "in the interest of justice" to transfer the cases to Massachusetts.

When the case came to the Supreme Court, this decision below was reversed and it was held that the cases might be transferred to Massachusetts. In reaching this result, the Supreme Court took a significant step. It held that when the cases were transferred to Massachusetts under section 1404 (a), they would still be Pennsylvania cases. The Federal Court sitting in Massachusetts should handle them in all respects as if it were a Federal court sitting in Pennsylvania and thus governed by the law of Pennsylvania under the *Erie* rule. Although the cases might be transferred, the transfer would have no effect on the applicable law.

Under this decision, all of the more than 150 actions arising out of the single accident can be now heard by the Federal Court in Massachusetts. This is obviously a convenience for many of the parties, and it should greatly simplify the proceedings, since most of the cases turn on the same factual questions, which can be heard together. But as to those cases originally filed in Massachusetts, the Federal district court will be sitting as a court of Massachusetts; while as to those cases originally filed in Pennsylvania, it will be sitting as a court of Pennsylvania. As such, it will look to the law of Pennsylvania on such questions as the standing of executors and administrators to sue, and the period of limitations. In looking to Pennsylvania law, it may find that, under that State's conflict of laws rule, the substantive law to be applied is that of Massachusetts. However, Massachusetts places a rather low ceiling on the amount of damages recoverable for wrongful death, and it is an unsettled question under Pennsylvania conflict of laws whether Pennsylvania would find it

against its public policy to accept this limit.[19] This question
of Pennsylvania law will have to be decided by the Federal
district court in Massachusetts, making use of such materials
on the law of Pennsylvania as it can find in the books, the
same materials that would be used by a Pennsylvania court in
Pennsylvania.

Thus, in the long run it may turn out that the more than
150 cases will all be heard together by the Federal district
court sitting in Massachusetts, but that it will reach one
result—on the same facts—in the more than 100 cases
originally filed in Massachusetts, and another result in the
more than 45 cases originally filed in Pennsylvania.

If you feel that this is an extremely complex legal system
you are surely right. If you feel that far too much time and
energy and expense are consumed in procedural questions
which are perhaps a bit esoteric and far removed from the
basic rights of the parties, I could not argue otherwise. It is,
for better or for worse, a part of the price we pay for a
Federal system, which though high, may in fact be worth the
cost. Perhaps some day we will work out ways to unify our
law and avoid a considerable part of these legal niceties. At
the present time, though, that day seems far away. Deep-
seated notions of States' rights make it seem doubtful that the
States will yield much of their law-making power to the
Federal government. And if each State retains its power to
make its own law in wide areas, diversity is the inevitable
result.

Except for the benefits we all receive from the Federal
system in our large and diverse country, the only beneficiaries

---

[19] The courts of New York have held that they would not accept the
Massachusetts limit. *Kilberg* v. *Northeast Airlines, Inc.*, 9 N.Y. 2d 34,
172 N.F. 2d 526, 211 N.Y.S. 2d 133 (1961).

are the lawyers. These problems involve a type of reasoning akin to that of scholasticism. Lawyers love these questions. Reams are written about them in law review articles and in judicial opinions. Students study them intensely in law school; and everybody debates them, and occasionally deplores them. But they are real. Practicing lawyers must consider them. Almost no lawsuit can be filed without considering carefully where it *can* be filed, and then where it *should* be filed to get the best result. This does not necessarily reduce justice to a lottery, but it does make the administration of justice more a matter of skill—very technical skill—than could be justified if one were originally setting up a system for the administration of justice. If the American lawyer could only get outside the confines of his own system, in which he is so largely entrapped from the beginning of his studies of government and of law, he would see how absurd it really is. When we are able to get such a perspective on ourselves we may be able to work out some better solutions for these problems.

THE AREA OF UNITY—FEDERAL LAW

Thus far, we have concentrated on the diversity of laws within the American Federal system, of which there is a considerable amount. But the United States would not be true to its name if there were not also an element of uniformity or, at least, of harmony provided for in our system. There are, in fact, a number of doctrines and devices in our laws and our Constitution for eliminating or minimizing many of the encumbering effects of disparate State laws. For present purposes, two notable illustrations should suffice. These are the doctrine of Federal preemption and the great

unifying force of the commerce clause of the Federal
Constitution.

Federal Preemption

Some areas of our law are exclusively the province of the
Federal government; in these areas, of course, diverse State
laws pose no serious problems. There are many areas, however, in which both the States and the Federal government
may have power to enact legislation. If several States have
exercised this power but the Federal government has not,
there is likely to be a diversity of laws in the area. But if
the Federal government does act, it may be found that it has
" preempted " or " occupied the field," so that any State legislation is displaced unless expressly permitted by Congress.
The doctrine of Federal preemption, then, may be a force for
eliminating diversity of laws in a given field throughout the
country. The constitutional mechanism for this displacement
of State law is the so-called Supremacy Clause, Article VI,
section 2, which provides that " This Constitution, and the
laws of the United States which shall be made in Pursuance
thereof . . . shall be the supreme Law of the Land; and the
Judges in every State shall be bound thereby. . . ."

There are many illustrations of Federal preemption, and I
will not try to review them here. There is one case—*Pennsylvania* v. *Nelson* [20]—which may serve as an example. Steve
Nelson, an acknowledged member of the Communist Party,
was indicted in Pennsylvania for violation of a Pennsylvania
statute proscribing sedition against the State government and
against the government of the United States. However, the

[20] 350 U.S. 497 (1956).

proof at the trial of his case involved only sedition against the United States. There is a comprehensive Federal statute, known as the Smith Act,[21] covering seditious conduct against the United States. Consequently, when the *Nelson* case came before the Supreme Court of Pennsylvania, that court held that Nelson could not be convicted under the Pennsylvania Act because the Federal statute had occupied the field. It thus superseded the Pennsylvania Sedition Act, as far as attempts to overthrow the government of the United States were concerned.[22] Since this decision involved the construction and effect of a Federal statute, the Supreme Court of the United States had jurisdiction to review the decision, and the prosecuting authorities of Pennsylvania sought and obtained a review in Washington.

The Supreme Court of the United States agreed with the Pennsylvania Supreme Court. It held that the field of sedition against the United States was one in which the Federal interest so predominated that State laws on the same subject, even if not in terms in conflict with the Federal law, could not be enforced. In addition, the Court noted that sporadic State regulation might hinder, rather than help, Federal authorities in their efforts to combat sedition on the national level.

Of course, this decision had its repercussions. The Supreme Court was denounced in Congress and in other quarters. Proposals were made to amend the Federal law so that the State laws could again be effective, but these have never resulted in legislation. This is a good example of the way in which our Supreme Court can become embroiled in

---

[21] 18 U.S.C. § 2385 (1958).
[22] *Nelson* v. *Pennsylvania*, 377 Pa. 58, 104 A.2d 133 (1955).

" politics " when it simply performs its duty of considering statute law and interpreting and applying it in the light of all the circumstances—these circumstances including the effective working of our Federal system. This is inevitable whenever a Court has to delimit the powers of two different Governmental agencies. Eventually our people understand this function, but sometimes there is a considerable outcry from certain quarters when the decision is first made. It is too bad that the Court has to face such criticism, often uninformed and unthinking. Yet in the decisions it makes in these and many other areas, the Court performs an essential function in making our Federal system work.

The Commerce Clause

One of the most important provisions of the American Constitution is one which has no counterpart in any aspect of the government of England, though the same general question does arise in other British countries, such as Canada and Australia. This provision is the Commerce Clause, Article I, section 8 of our Constitution, which provides that " Congress shall have Power . . . To regulate Commerce with foreign Nations and among the several States, and with the Indian Tribes." These are simple words, but they have had far-reaching effect. It is not too much to say, I think, that these words have had more to do with making us a Nation than any other provision of the Constitution.

In the earliest days, there was not a great deal of commerce between the States—interstate commerce, we call it— and development of the Commerce Clause was rather slow. But this changed rapidly with the coming of the steamboat.

The first great case was *Gibbons* v. *Ogden*,[23] decided in 1824 in a famous opinion by Chief Justice Marshall. This case involved a grant held by Ogden from the legislature of New York, giving him the exclusive right to employ steam vessels in the navigation of the Hudson River, within the jurisdiction of New York. For a part of its course, the Hudson River is the boundary between New York and New Jersey, and another steamboat operator, Gibbons, operated two vessels on the river between New York City and Elizabethtown, New Jersey. For a part of this trip, Gibbons' steamboats travelled in New York waters, and this was in violation of Ogden's exclusive right of steam navigation upon the New York part of the Hudson.

Thus we had a direct clash between State power, represented by the grant made to Ogden by the legislature of New York, applicable within New York, and the power of Congress under the Commerce Clause, to regulate commerce "among the several States." It should be noted, though, that Congress had not, to any great extent, undertaken to exercise its power as applied to this particular situation. Gibbons did have a Federal license to be employed in the coasting trade under an Act of Congress of 1793. But there was no Federal statute which expressly invalidated the exclusive grant made by the State of New York for Ogden's use of New York waters.

Ogden sued in the New York courts, and obtained an injunction against Gibbons' operations in New York territory.[24] Gibbons then brought the case to the Supreme Court

---

23 9 Wheat. 1 (U.S. 1824). See Warren, *The Supreme Court in United States History*, Vol. 1, Ch. 15 (Rev. ed. 1932). For a comparative study of the basic problems, see Smith, *The Commerce Power in Canada and the United States* (Butterworth's 1963).

24 *Ogden* v. *Gibbons*, 4 Johns. Ch. 150 (N.Y. 1819).

of the United States, contending that the New York Act was repugnant to the Commerce Clause of the Federal Constitution. In one of the great landmark cases in our Constitutional history, the Court, through Chief Justice Marshall, sustained Gibbons' contentions.

In reaching this decision, the Court relied to some extent on Gibbons' general Federal license for coastwise navigation. It seems likely, though, that the Court would have reached the same result even if Gibbons had claimed under no Federal statute, but merely rested on the ground that (at least without the permission of Congress) the State had no right to prohibit his navigation in interstate commerce. It is now thoroughly established that the Federal Congress may, through protective enactment or through silence,[25] protect, regulate, or prohibit any form of interstate commerce, and that the States may not, without the permission of Congress, exclude interstate commerce in the guise of regulating their internal affairs.

The cases in this field include not only prohibitions of interstate commerce by the States, and efforts to regulate or limit interstate commerce, but also various State taxes on interstate commerce. This is a highly intricate field, in which the last word has not been said. Congress has recently entered the area by passing a statute which provides that certain types of conduct by a business enterprise within the borders of a State may not be utilized by the State to subject the business to State taxation. The validity of this statute has recently been sustained by the Supreme Court of Louisiana,[26] and it will no doubt come before the Supreme Court of the United States before long. It is obvious that this

---

[25] See Biklé, " The Silence of Congress," 41 *Harv.L.Rev.* 200 (1927).
[26] *International Shoe Co.* v. *Cocreham*, 164 So.2d 314 (La. 1964).

type of case, too, involves the Court in "political questions," though its sole function is to interpret and apply the Constitution. Yet its decision will either have to strike down a State's attempt to impose a tax, or invalidate an Act of Congress. Either result is likely to result in sharp criticism from political quarters, State or Federal.

In recent years, Congress has greatly increased the scope of its legislation under the Commerce Clause, and after some initial difficulty the Court has upheld the Federal power. In early cases under the antitrust laws, the Court had held that manufacturing was not commerce. In *United States* v. *E. C. Knight Co.*,[27] the United States brought an action against a number of sugar refining companies for a conspiracy to monopolize, and the actual monopolization, of the manufacture and sale of refined sugar in the United States. A majority of the Supreme Court (only the first Justice Harlan dissenting) held that even if the existence of a monopoly in manufacture were established, the United States could not maintain the action, since manufacture was not within the regulatory power of Congress under the Commerce Clause. It was considered to be an activity purely internal to the States in which the factories were located, even though the articles manufactured were intended for export to another State.

In more recent years, however, as the economy of the country has grown and become more complex and interdependent, the Court has come to the conclusion that the power of Congress to regulate interstate commerce is almost unlimited, that is, that there are almost no actions within a State which do not "affect commerce" in some way sufficient

[27] 156 U.S. 1 (1895).

for Congress to regulate them if it wishes to do so. Perhaps the greatest stretch in this direction was taken in the case of *Wickard* v. *Filburn*,[28] which involved the Agricultural Adjustment Act of 1938. Under this statute the Federal Secretary of Agriculture was authorized to establish a national acreage allotment for certain agricultural production, and (subject to approval by farmers in a referendum) a national marketing quota, when the acreage allotment proved too large to keep production down to a reasonable level. The quotas so established would then be allocated to individual farms. Excess production on any farm, from excess acreage, was made subject to a penalty, and this was applied even if the excess production was intended to be used, and was in fact used, purely for consumption on the farm where it was produced. Despite the local effect of such production, the statute was held to be within the Federal power to regulate interstate commerce. This conclusion was reached through an analysis, essentially economic in content, of the general agricultural situation in the country. Under this analysis, it was found that agricultural production for home consumption "exerts a substantial economic effect on interstate commerce,"[29] and that this was enough to enable Congress to regulate or control it.

Although the *Wickard* case represents perhaps the high water mark of interstate commerce, the broad approach exemplified in that decision has been followed in many other cases sustaining Acts of Congress which have to a considerable extent transformed our economy and our society. Thus, in *Steward Machine Co.* v. *Davis*,[30] the Court sustained the

[28] 317 U.S. 111 (1942).
[29] *Id*. at 125.
[30] 301 U.S. 548 (1937).

Social Security Tax, which provides both for Old Age and Survivors Insurance and also for Unemployment Insurance. In *National Labor Relations Board* v. *Jones & Laughlin Steel Co.*,[31] it upheld the National Labor Relations Act, which establishes a Code of Fair Labor Practices on a nationwide basis, covering industries which " affect commerce." The Act also sets up the National Labor Relations Board as a tribunal to hear cases where violations of the Act are charged and with power to enforce the Act. And in *United States* v. *Darby*,[32] the Court upheld the Fair Labor Standards Act, which prohibits child labor, regulates the hours of labor in all industries " affecting commerce," and provides for time-and-a-half pay where overtime is worked.

It may be pointed out that without Federal action in these fields, it would have been very difficult for the individual States to regulate hours of labor and working conditions. For it is very hard for one State to maintain statutes improving working conditions if its neighboring States do not follow suit. The goods of each of the States are in competition with each other, and if one State enacts legislation which increases the costs of doing business there above those of other States, then the high-cost States will lose business and will be confronted with unemployment. These are problems which we have at last come to see can only be resolved on a National basis. The Commerce Clause, as it has lately been construed by the Supreme Court, has made this possible.

The development of the Commerce Clause illustrates the way in which some parts of the Constitution may rightly receive a different construction in one era than they do in

31 301 U.S. 1 (1937).
32 312 U.S. 100 (1941).

another, and shows how important it is that the Supreme
Court has and, from time to time, exercises the power to
re-examine its earlier decisions. In the early nineteenth
century, interstate commerce was not a very important factor
in our economy. Most matters were truly of primarily local
interest, and it was appropriate to adopt a fairly narrow
interpretation of the power of Congress to regulate commerce.
But in the middle of the twentieth century the situation is
completely changed. Practically all business is done on a
nationwide basis. During the course of a single day, every-
one uses materials which have been produced in other States,
eats food which has come from other States, and does acts
himself which have their eventual impact in other States.
What was once essentially a series of local problems has
rightly become a national problem. Where there was little
need for Congress to have power in the past, except in what
might be called gross cases, it is essential that Congress now
have sweeping powers effective on a nationwide basis. All
this is possible through the Commerce Clause as it is re-
construed from time to time in the light of changing
circumstances and the changing nature of the economy. In
this way, as I have said, the Supreme Court has enabled us to
become and to remain a nation. Without the Commerce
Clause, we would have had what has been called the
Balkanization of the United States.

In this respect, our Founding Fathers proved to be more
far-seeing, I think, than did the draftsmen of the British North
America Act and the Commonwealth of Australia Constitu-
tion Act, who, while making use of some parts of the
American Constitution, did not adopt the Commerce Clause.
The allocation in Canada of power over specific areas, such

as banking, to the Federal Government has not been as effective in actual operation as is the general power given to Congress by the Commerce Clause. In Australia, the problem was resolved by Section 92 of the Australian Constitution, which provides that "Trade, commerce, and intercourse between the several states shall be absolutely free." This has a certain allure, on first reading. However, as interpreted and applied, it comes fairly close to saying that neither the states of Australia nor the Federal government there have power to regulate commerce among the States. This leads to a sort of vacuum of power, which may have been attractive in 1900, but which does not, I think, fit very well in 1964. It may well be that the Commerce Clause is the most important single conception in the United States Constitution. It deserves to be considered carefully whenever a Federal constitution is being drafted.

INTERPLAY OF STATE AND FEDERAL COURTS

With all the diversity of laws inherent in the structure of the American Federal system, we have seen that the laws and Constitution of the central government may be a force for unification and harmonization. But these unifying Federal laws do not apply themselves; the success or failure of these laws to bring a degree of unity to the nation depends in large measure on the effectiveness of the courts which administer them. Here again, we must turn our attention to the dual system of courts in the United States. For the Federal laws and constitutional rules, though theoretically of uniform application, are administered and interpreted in both Federal and State tribunals. Their ultimate arbiter is the United States Supreme Court, but that Court is an extremely busy one. Thus, before the highest court in the land has a chance to speak on a matter, a Federal rule designed to apply uniformly throughout the nation may in fact be given varied interpretations by the several State and intermediate Federal courts which consider it.

Direct Federal Review of State Decisions

As the situation just described is perhaps most acute in the area of fundamental constitutional liberties, let me illustrate the interworkings of the Federal and State courts by two recent cases in that area. First, there is the case of *Gideon* v. *Wainwright*,[33] decided by the United States Supreme Court on March 18, 1963. The issue was the right of an indigent person accused of a noncapital crime to be represented by court-appointed counsel. Gideon was accused of breaking and entering a store and stealing certain items, including money. This was a felony in the State of Florida, where the case arose. At his trial in the Florida State court, Gideon requested that counsel be appointed to represent him, but the request was refused, and since he was without funds, he conducted the defense himself. After a full trial, he was convicted; his conviction was upheld on appeal to the Florida Supreme Court, and he was placed in a prison operated by the State of Florida.

One might suppose that would be the end of the matter. Gideon had presented his case to the appropriate Florida courts, and he had lost. Moreover, the decision of the Supreme Court of Florida on this matter was in accord with a previous decision of the Supreme Court of the United

[33] 372 U.S. 335 (1963).

States. In 1942, in the case of *Betts* v. *Brady*,[34] that Court had held that the Constitution does not require a State to furnish counsel except in capital cases or in cases where there were exceptional circumstances, such as a defendant of low-grade intelligence, or issues of unusual complexity.

But Gideon was persistent. He wrote a letter to the Supreme Court of the United States in Washington, seeking review of the decision of the Supreme Court of Florida. In such cases, the Supreme Court of the United States has jurisdiction only over a question arising under the Federal Constitution, and this jurisdiction is discretionary only. The Court reviews only those cases it feels are of special importance. When the papers that Gideon had prepared for himself reached the Justices, they voted to grant a writ of certiorari so that the record in the lower court might be brought before them, and they appointed eminent counsel to represent the defendant. In the order granting the writ, the Court expressly invited counsel " to discuss the following in their briefs and oral argument: ' Should this Court's holding in *Betts* v. *Brady* . . . be reconsidered? ' "

Now, how could this be? Would not any soundly administered judicial system regard a case like *Betts* v. *Brady* as stare decisis? Why should the Court, on its own motion, invite reconsideration? These are not easy questions to answer, but, in some ways, the answer goes to the very root of the American judicial system. For *Betts* v. *Brady* was a decision in the field of constitutional law. There was no power in any legislature to change it, and constitutional amendment is a very long and difficult process. Yet the Supreme Court was responsible for the rule in that case; and

[34] 316 U.S. 455 (1942).

if the Court came to feel that the earlier decision had been erroneous, its responsibility in a very real sense continued.

In the years since *Betts* v. *Brady* was decided, the great majority of the American States had voluntarily decided to provide counsel for defendants accused of serious offenses. Actually, in 1963, when the *Gideon* case was decided, thirty-five States provided for the assignment of counsel, with varying procedures, some of great and some of less effectiveness. But there were still States which did not provide counsel except as required by the rule of *Betts* v. *Brady* in capital cases and in cases where there were extraordinary circumstances. Florida was one of these States; and most of the rest of them were in the deep south. Incidentally, Gideon was not a Negro, and the case has no particular racial implications.

After the printed briefs were filed, and the case was argued by counsel, the Supreme Court did overrule *Betts* v. *Brady* and held that Gideon was entitled to counsel at his trial. This result was reached on the basis of the Fourteenth Amendment to the Constitution of the United States, adopted in 1866, which provides that no State shall " deprive any person of life, liberty, or property, without due process of law; nor deny to any person within its jurisdiction the equal protection of the laws." As you can see, this language is quite general. There is also a provision in the Sixth Amendment which says that " In all criminal prosecutions, the accused shall enjoy the right . . . to have the Assistance of Counsel for his defence." But the history of this provision shows that it is applicable only to trials in the Federal Courts. Moreover, it is doubtful whether in its origin it was intended to assure a defendant that he could have counsel assigned to him for his defense. It was probably intended to provide that where a defendant had his own counsel, he could be represented, contrary to the common law and the rule which remained in effect in England until 1836. But in 1938, in a case called *Johnson* v. *Zerbst*,[35] the Supreme Court had decided that this provision of the Sixth Amendment did mean that a defendant was entitled to have counsel assigned to him when he was tried in a Federal court. As time went on, it came to seem more and more anomalous that a different rule should apply when a State, rather than a Federal, crime was charged. And more and more it became apparent that the right to the effective assistance of counsel was, in our society today, one of those fundamental rights which are the essence of the guaranty of "due process of law" in the Fourteenth Amendment.

So an obscure prisoner in Florida, with several criminal convictions in the past, helped to make new law in the United States. After the Supreme Court's decision, he was tried again in the Florida trial court. This time counsel was assigned to him; and this time he was acquitted by a jury. Thus the right given to him turned out to be more than a formality.[36]

One of the questions which followed in the wake of the *Gideon* case was the effect of that decision on the convictions of persons who had been tried without counsel before that case was decided, where the failure to assign counsel was in accordance with the rule established in *Betts* v. *Brady*. Although the Supreme Court has not decided this question, some lower courts have regarded the *Gideon* decision as

[35] 304 U.S. 458 (1938).
[36] For a full discussion of the *Gideon* case, in popular terms, see Lewis, *Gideon's Trumpet* (1964). See also Clayton, *The Making of Justice—The Supreme Court in Action* 131–138, 228–235, 292–293 (1964).

applicable in all such cases. As a result, in the State of Florida alone some thousands of prisoners have been retried, and over a thousand have been released, either because of acquittal on the new trial or because their cases were dismissed since witnesses were no longer available. This is of course a serious matter, but not so serious, in our view, as the establishment of the rule that every defendant charged with a serious crime is entitled to the aid of counsel. This is now the rule in every court in the country, but it took a long time and a Supreme Court decision to make it so.

Collateral Federal Review of State Decisions

Although two different sets of courts were involved in the *Gideon* case, the procedure there was fairly simple; Gideon obtained direct review of the decision of the Florida court by mailing his papers to the Supreme Court in Washington. That the interplay of State and Federal courts needed to effectuate a rule of Federal constitutional law is not always so simple was painfully demonstrated in the recent case of *Fay* v. *Noia*,[37] decided on the same day as *Gideon* v. *Wainwright*.

The almost unbelievably complicated story began in 1942, when three criminal defendants named Noia, Caminito and Bonino were convicted in a New York State court of murder committed in connection with an armed robbery and were sentenced to life imprisonment. None of the defendants took the stand in his own defense, and the only evidence against each of them was the separate confession which each had signed while in custody.

Noia did not appeal his conviction. This was partly because he was not sure of the result and did not want to

[37] 372 U.S. 391 (1963).

waste any more of his family's already depleted funds. It was, too, partly because he feared that if his appeal were successful, and he obtained a new trial, he might be sentenced to death rather than to life imprisonment if he were again convicted. The trial judge had indicated that he had seriously considered the death penalty for Noia, who had a previous criminal record; and it was he who had apparently fired the fatal shot.

Caminito and Bonino did appeal their convictions. They were at first unsuccessful. The convictions were affirmed by the Appellate Division of the Supreme Court of New York,[38] and by the New York Court of Appeals,[39] which is the highest court in that State. Under the New York practice, a prisoner who has taken his case to the Court of Appeals may at any time file a petition for a rehearing of his appeal, and Caminito did so twice, unsuccessfully.[40] Following the second unsuccessful attempt, Caminito filed a petition for certiorari with the Supreme Court of the United States. But the Court, exercising its discretion, denied the petition.[41] During the same period, Bonino filed one petition for rehearing with the New York Court of Appeals, which was denied,[42] and a petition for certiorari with the United States Supreme Court, which also was denied.[43]

Though he had brought his case before the highest court of the State three times and the highest court of the nation

[38] *People* v. *Caminito*, 265 App.Div. 960, 38 N.Y.S. 2d 1018 (1942).
[39] *People* v. *Bonino*, 291 N.Y. 541, 50 N.E. 2d 654 (1943).
[40] *People* v. *Caminito*, 297 N.Y. 882, 79 N.E. 2d 277 (1948); and *People* v. *Caminito*, 307 N.Y. 686, 120 N.E. 2d 857 (1954).
[41] *Caminito* v. *New York*, 348 U.S. 839 (1954).
[42] *People* v. *Bonino*, 296 N.Y. 1004, 73 N.E. 2d 579 (1947).
[43] *Bonino* v. *New York*, 333 U.S. 849 (1948).

once, Caminito still persisted. He filed a petition for a writ of habeas corpus in the Federal district court for the Northern District of New York, within whose jurisdiction he was being held. To invoke the jurisdiction of this court, it was necessary for Caminito to raise a Federal question. He was able to meet this requirement by contending that the confession used to convict him had been coerced by the police. If his contention could be borne out, it would show that he had been convicted in violation of the Federal Constitution. For a conviction based upon a coerced confession constitutes a deprivation of " life, liberty, or property, without due process of law," contrary to the Fourteenth Amendment.[44] The question whether a confession was coerced is a Federal question, which a Federal court is required to determine, if the issue is properly raised. No prior determination of any State court on this question is binding on the Federal judiciary; otherwise the State courts might have the final word in judging the actions of State officers against Federal constitutional criteria.

Passing on Caminito's petition for habeas corpus, the Federal district court held that the confession was not coerced and, thus, that no Federally guaranteed rights were violated.[45] But on appeal, the United States Court of Appeals for the Second Circuit, which sits in New York, reversed the lower court decision. It held that the confession was coerced, and it ordered that Caminito either be given a new trial or be

---

[44] For applications of this rule, see *Watts* v. *Indiana*, 338 U.S. 49 (1949); *Ashcraft* v. *Tennessee*, 322 U.S. 143 (1944).

[45] *United States, ex rel. Caminito* v. *Murphy*, 127 F.Supp. 689 (N.D.N.Y. 1955).

released.[46] In effect, this ruling applied to Bonino and Noia as well, since all three statements were obtained under the same circumstances. A writ of certiorari was once again sought from the Supreme Court of the United States—this time by the authorities of the State of New York—and once again the writ was refused.[47]

Under the circumstances, the State was unable to retry Caminito. As for Bonino, he filed a new petition for rehearing to the New York Court of Appeals. This time the rehearing was granted, and the New York tribunal followed the decision of the Federal court in Caminito's case and ordered Bonino to be either retried or released.[48] In this case also, retrial was no longer feasible. Thus, after fourteen years in prison, Caminito and Bonino were free men.

Only Noia remained in jail. The sole relevant difference between his case and the cases of his two companions was that they had appealed their original convictions, while he had not. This difference may seem slight, but it proved crucial under New York procedure. In the first place, it meant that no petition for rehearing was open to Noia. Thus, he proceeded upon a writ of coram nobis and was, in fact, successful in having the lower New York State court set his conviction aside.[49] But the State appealed this

---

[46] *United States, ex rel. Caminito* v. *Murphy*, 222 F. 2d 698 (2d Cir. 1955). The opinion shows that there was no police brutality. But Caminito (and the others) were questioned almost continuously for 27 hours. They were not arraigned for 42 hours. They were held incommunicado, though relatives and their lawyer tried to see them; and police detectives falsely identified them. The opinion by Judge Frank is an eloquent statement of the necessity of sound police practices.

[47] *Murphy* v. *United States, ex rel. Caminito*, 350 U.S. 896 (1955).

[48] *People* v. *Bonino*, 1 N.Y. 2d 752, 135 N.E. 2d 51, 152 N.Y.S. 2d 298 (1956).

[49] *People* v. *Noia*, 3 Misc. 2d 447, 158 N.Y.S. 2d 683 (King's Cty.Ct. 1956).

decision to the New York Appellate Division, which reversed the lower court. It held that Noia's failure to appeal in 1942 —fifteen years earlier—made his original conviction res judicata on all matters in issue and deprived him of the right to seek relief at any later time.[50]   The New York Court of Appeals affirmed this decision,[51] and the United States Supreme Court, as a matter of discretion, you will recall, denied a petition for certiorari.[52]

Noia then sought relief on habeas corpus from the Federal district court as had Caminito, but again his earlier failure to appeal came back to haunt him. It is a well-settled rule— of comity, it is called—that before a Federal court will act on a petition for habeas corpus, the defendant must have exhausted all remedies available to him under State law. This rule is a reflection of the niceties of a Federal system. The State courts have the basic responsibility for administering their criminal law, including the disposition of Federal questions involved in cases before them. It is thought to be a good rule of intergovernmental relations that the State courts be given full opportunity to pass on such Federal questions before any of the Federal courts will intervene. Thus the Federal district court denied Noia's petition for habeas corpus. It held that his original failure to appeal constituted both a waiver by him of any grounds he had for objecting to the conviction and a failure to exhaust available State remedies.[53]   But this decision was reversed by the

---

[50] *People* v. *Noia,* 4 App.Div. 2d 698, 163 N.Y.S. 2d 796 (1957).
[51] *People* v. *Caminito,* 3 N.Y. 2d 596, 148 N.E. 2d 139, 170 N.Y.S. 2d 799 (1958).
[52] *Noia* v. *New York,* 357 U.S. 905 (1958).
[53] *United States, ex rel. Noia* v. *Fay,* 183 F.Supp. 222 (S.D.N.Y. 1960).

United States Court of Appeals for the Second Circuit,[54] and on a writ of certiorari sought by the State of New York, the United States Supreme Court upheld the Court of Appeals.[55] Thus Noia, too, was finally set free, twenty-one years after his original conviction!

The Supreme Court held that Federal habeas corpus was available to a State prisoner who had failed to appeal his original conviction. The requirement that State remedies be exhausted meant merely the exhaustion of such remedies as were available at the time the petition for habeas corpus was filed. So Noia's application in the New York courts for a writ of coram nobis was sufficient exhaustion of State remedies. The Court went on to say, further, that under the unusual circumstances of this case, where both of the prisoner's co-defendants had been set free, and where the only evidence offered against the defendant was a confession which was now held and conceded to have been coerced, the prisoner should not be barred on the ground that he had waived his objections by failing to appeal.

Thus ended this almost incredible saga—incredible for its procedural voluminousness and complexity, incredible for the long time and many stages which were required to resolve the essentially simple fact situation. I would hope you understand that *Noia's* case is not typical. Indeed, I have picked it as a curious as well as a horrible example. It does show, though, how the fact that we have both State and Federal jurisdictions, which rightly and naturally show a certain amount of deference to each other, leads sometimes to a sort of legal battledore and shuttlecock, with cases bouncing

---

[54] *United States, ex rel. Noia* v. *Fay*, 300 F. 2d 345 (2d Cir. 1962).
[55] *Fay* v. *Noia*, 372 U.S. 391 (1963).

back and forth almost endlessly between the State and the Federal jurisdictions. We ought to work out a better system for handling these matters, and perhaps some day we will. One of the difficulties arises from the fact that our country is so large that the Supreme Court of the United States simply cannot hear all of the cases which are brought to it. In the several matters which were overall involved in *Noia's* case, the Supreme Court denied certiorari four times—the first of these in 1948—before it finally decided the case in 1963, fifteen years later. But the case probably was not " ripe " for decision in 1948. I do not know what facts appeared on Bonino's first effort to get his case heard by the highest court, but they may have been very inadequately presented in that record. Moreover, as a matter of sheer practicality, the Supreme Court can only hear a very small percentage of the cases which are brought to its door.

In this situation, the solution might be that the lower courts should do a better job. They, too, have their problems. It will be remembered that Noia himself did not appeal his conviction, and made no effort to have his case heard further until 1956, after he had been in jail for fourteen years.

What moral can be drawn from *Fay* v. *Noia?* The answer is not entirely clear. In part, the case illustrates an improvement in our standards of administration of criminal justice which has slowly been developing over the past twenty to twenty-five years, under the leadership of the Supreme Court. Gideon's case is another example of this. I have no doubt that a considerable measure of compulsion was used to obtain the confessions from Noia, Caminito and Bonino.

Just how much is not important; any coercion was too much. Yet, in 1942 this was probably a fairly frequent police practice, and not much was done about it except in extreme cases. By 1963, under the Supreme Court's leadership, standards in this area have markedly improved. Police officers now generally know that conduct of this sort will not be condoned, and that it will jeopardize convictions. As a result, they prepare their cases better. Witnesses are found, and a case like that of Noia, Caminito, and Bonino would not be tried today with the confession as the only evidence offered by the prosecution.

On the other hand, the *Noia* case is, in many ways, a sad commentary on our procedural system, on the complexity of our law, and on our administration of criminal justice. It is too bad that it happened; and it is too bad that it took so long and required so many proceedings, bouncing back and forth between the State and Federal courts, to straighten it out. Nevertheless, it does illustrate the almost infinite care and patience of our system, and this may have some merit. There were many days in court, but eventually justice was done.

CONCLUSION

In this Chapter, I have been able to touch on only a few aspects of the Constitutional and Federal problems which arise under the Constitution of the United States. I believe that none of the cases mentioned has any counterpart in the law and jurisprudence of England. You may well be saying, Why does he bother us with this? What interest do we have in this complicated recital of a series of problems which are, so fortunately, unknown to us?

For one thing, I want to show you how the common law method and approach has adapted itself to new problems, and to new situations. Novel as these questions are, we attack them in the way we have learned to proceed under the legal system we have inherited from England. Constitutional and Federal questions are in one sense a world apart. But in another they are still a part of the fabric of the common law, peculiarly subject to analysis and resolution by the techniques of the common law.

Another purpose is that you may understand us and our system a little better. Undoubtedly our system is too complicated. If we could start over we would surely try to simplify it in various ways. But there are many reasons in history and in human nature which mean that we cannot start over, and cannot very well change what we now have. So we have to live with it and make it work. Though you may rejoice that you do not have similar problems, it may be desirable for you to have some understanding of what we are doing when we have to deal with these questions.

And finally, I have tried to illustrate that our Courts, though inevitably having to decide questions with great political implications, are not acting politically, and are not engaging in politics when they decide such questions. They are simply performing their duty in deciding the questions of law which inevitably arise under a constitutional and Federal system. They may do that task well, or do it badly. They may even, in some case, allow an extraneous factor to affect their judgment. But in this task, they are not acting differently from other judges. They are performing judicial work, construing and applying Constitutional and statutory provisions to the end that controversies between men and men, and between men and their governments, may be rightly resolved. What they do they do in the spirit of the common law, though the questions they have to decide may be ones which would have startled the judges who formulated the common law.

CHAPTER 5

THE PROBLEM OF CIVIL RIGHTS—
ITS LEGAL ASPECTS

HISTORICALLY, the white peoples of Europe and America have been neither very generous nor very successful in dealing with the other races of the world. The United States today has inherited the problems which naturally arise out of these policies of the past. My approach to the questions of civil rights will be largely from a legal point of view, though in the larger sense the problems are moral rather than legal. Yet the law has played its part in bringing them on, and it has contributed to their solution.

SLAVERY AND THE COMMON LAW

Slavery began in what is now the United States late in August, 1619. John Rolfe, the secretary and recorder of the Virginia colony reported that at this time "there came to Virginia 'a dutch man of warre that sold us twenty Negers.'"[1] At first the lot of the Negro was not a heavy one. He could buy his freedom, much as in the case of an indentured servant. It was not until 1661 that the legal status of slavery existed in Virginia. It is perhaps not inappropriate to point out that this was then British territory, with its laws

---

[1] Davie, *Negroes in American Society* 17 (1949), quoted in U.S. Comm'n on Civil Rights, *Freedom to the Free* 7 (1963). See also Phillips, *American Negro Slavery* (1959); Woodson & Wesley, *The Negro in Our History* (1962).

subject to approval and rejection by the Crown or Government in Westminster. When Lord Mansfield decided *Somerset* v. *Stewart* [2] in 1772 denying the validity of slavery in England, it did not occur to anyone that this rule should be equally applicable in other British territories. Great Britain did not abolish the slave trade until 1808,[3] and slavery was not abolished in all British territories until 1834.[4] This was a commendable achievement, but it came too late to do us any good.

Slavery was, of course, not confined to North America. It first appeared in the islands of the West Indies, and it was extensively utilized in the Spanish and Portuguese settlements of Central and South America. But here we find at once a significant difference. For slavery in Latin territories was rarely a demoralizing influence. The colonizers took with them their legal systems, which were derived from that of Rome; and Roman law had extensive provisions relating to slavery. South American law preserved the legal personality of the slave. He could own property and could purchase his freedom at a fixed price. Moreover, the influential Catholic Church was interested in the souls of slaves; and, as marriage was a sacrament, marriage among slaves was recognized and sacrosanct. As Charles E. Silberman has said, " Because Spanish and Portuguese law saw slavery as a misfortune that could happen to anyone, and because it insisted that the slave had a soul and mind and personality of his own, the opprobrium Americans attached to color never developed. . . . South American whites never seriously maintained that a Negro

---

[2] Lofft 1, 21 How.St.Tr. 1 (1772).
[3] 47 Geo. 3, c. 36. See Greenidge, *Slavery* 127–38 (1958).
[4] 3 & 4 Will. 4, c. 73.

slave was *incapable* of being free. On the contrary, the freed slaves enjoyed the same legal rights as the white man and on the whole the same social status." [5]

But the law in the English colonies developed quite differently. There was no common law of slavery to carry forward. The ancient common law of villeinage or serfdom had disappeared and was not thought to be applicable in any way. The analogy which was developed was that of the law of chattels. A man's bed and chair and clothes are his, to do with as he pleases; and the same is true with his horse or his cow. As far as the common law is concerned, he can burn up his chair, or beat his horse or cow. The only protection for the animal is the owner's self interest. Since it is his property, presumably he will not do anything to impair or destroy it. And so, in the common law as it developed in the American colonies, a slave became a chattel. He had no rights against his owner. More than that, the slave had no personality as far as the law was concerned, no more than the owner's horse or cow.

This legal status was of course degrading in the extreme, and it had tremendous consequences. A slave had no father, as far as the law was concerned, and he could not marry. Whatever marriage was recognised was simply due to the generosity and compassion of the master. Slave families could be broken up with no hindrance from the law; a slave mother could be separated from her children. The slave lost, too, all trace of social or moral status, and the relationship between the races became fixed as one of superiority-inferiority. Slaves could not sue their masters, even for the worst abuse. Except

[5] Silberman, *Crisis in Black and White* 87 (1964).

in the most extreme cases the law imposed no sanction on the slave-owner for mistreatment of a slave; and even where there was a sanction, the slave could not testify, so the sanction was likely to be ineffective. Thus, for generations, inferiority was ground into the members of the colored race; and the white race, with varying degrees of compunction and responsibility, accepted a position of superiority. It is hardly surprising that it has been extremely difficult for some white persons to accept Negroes as fully equal members of their society, or that Negroes have not always been ready to accept the full measure of responsibility. The extent to which this situation goes back to our common law heritage has been noted, but perhaps not generally appreciated.

Civil War Amendments

Without repeating history, I need only mention that agitation for the abolition of slavery began in the eighteenth century, and became stronger in the nineteenth. Few problems in all history have aroused greater passions. In our country the course led eventually to a terrible Civil War, fought ostensibly to " save the Union." But one cannot overlook the fact that the essential background, the *causa sine qua non*, was the continued existence of slavery. When the war was ended, slavery had been abolished in the United States, and within a few years three important amendments to the Constitution were adopted. These are what have made the problem today a constitutional and legal problem, as well as the moral problem which it inevitably is. It will be helpful, I think, to give here the text of the principal portions of these Amendments:

Thirteenth Amendment, adopted in 1865

> Neither slavery nor involuntary servitude, except as a punishment for crime whereof the party shall have been duly convicted, shall exist within the United States, or any place subject to their jurisdiction.

Fourteenth Amendment, adopted in 1868

> All persons born or naturalized in the United States, and subject to the jurisdiction thereof, are citizens of the United States and of the State wherein they reside. No State shall make or enforce any law which shall abridge the privileges or immunities of citizens of the United States; nor shall any State deprive any person of life, liberty, or property, without due process of law; nor deny to any person within its jurisdiction the equal protection of the laws.

Fifteenth Amendment, adopted in 1870

> The right of citizens of the United States to vote shall not be denied or abridged by the United States or by any State on account of race, color, or previous condition of servitude.

And, with respect to each of these Amendments, it was further provided that—

> The Congress shall have power to enforce this article by appropriate legislation.

Occasionally it is contended that these Amendments, and the Fourteenth Amendment in particular, were not validly adopted, in that the ratifications of some of the States were coerced. This is, I think, a symptom of the larger problem with which the country is confronted, namely, that a large part of the South has simply refused to accept the settlement of the question which was wrought by the Civil War. That war was a great tragedy. That it should have accomplished so little after a period of a hundred years is a comparable tragedy.

The sad fact is that many people, especially in the South, are still fighting the Civil War. William Faulkner has caught this point in his *Absalom, Absalom!* where Shreve McCannon, speaking in 1910, says [6]:

> "We don't live among defeated grandfathers and freed slaves (or have I got it backward and was it your folks that are free and the niggers that lost?) and bullets in the dining room table and such, to be always reminding us to never forget. What is it? something you live and breathe in like air? a kind of vacuum filled with wraithlike and indomitable anger and pride and glory at and in happenings that occurred and ceased fifty years ago? a kind of entailed birthright father and son and father and son of never forgiving General Sherman, so that forevermore as long as your children's children produce children you won't be anything but a descendant of a long line of colonels killed in Pickett's charge at Manassas?"

It is true that the Civil War ended the institution of slavery. But we are still dealing with vestiges of slavery, and the great hopes which were raised at the conclusion of the War and which were embodied in the sweeping language of the Civil War Amendments to the Constitution have continuously eluded our grasp.

JUDICIAL INTERPRETATION OF THE AMENDMENTS

Early Backward Steps

For this sad result the Supreme Court bears a considerable measure of responsibility. Though there were many details

[6] Ch. 9, par. 7, p. 361 (Modern Library ed. 1936).

and developments, I will here make reference to three decisions of the Court, in the latter part of the nineteenth century, which form an important part of the background for our problem in the twentieth century.

The first of these goes by the name of the *Civil Rights Cases.*[7] It involved a statute passed by Congress in 1875, which provided—

> That all persons within the jurisdiction of the United States shall be entitled to the full and equal enjoyment of the accommodations, advantages, facilities, and privileges of inns, public conveyances on land or water, theatres, and other places of public amusement; . . . regardless of any previous condition of servitude.[8]

The statute also provided penalties for its violation, which could be recovered by the person aggrieved, or by indictment, the two remedies to be mutually exclusive.

Seven years after its enactment, a number of cases involving this statute came before the Supreme Court. Only one of them came from a Southern State. This involved a refusal of a railroad to seat a Negro woman in a parlor car in Tennessee. The other cases arose in California, Kansas, Missouri and New York, and involved refusal of accommodations at an inn, or in a theater.

In the *Civil Rights Cases,* the Supreme Court held that the Act of 1875 was beyond the power of Congress. In construing the statute, the Court did not refer to the power of Congress to regulate commerce among the several States. It did note that Congress placed no explicit reliance in the statute itself on the Fourteenth Amendment, but the Court gave a

[7] 109 U.S. 3 (1883).
[8] Act of March 1, 1875, 18 Stat. 336.

literal interpretation to that Amendment, which as we have seen provides that " No State " shall deny the privileges and immunities of citizenship, nor deny to any person due process of law or equal protection of the laws. This means, said the Court, that the Fourteenth Amendment gives Congress power only with respect to State action. In the cases before the Court, all of the discriminatory actions had been by private citizens, with respect to private premises or accommodations. For Congress to forbid such actions by private persons was, said the Court, beyond its power, or, as you would say, *ultra vires*. The States had power to pass such statutes, and many States in the North or West have done so. But there are no Southern States which have enacted anti-discrimination statutes.

The opinion of the Court in the *Civil Rights Cases* was written by Mr. Justice Bradley. Referring to the lot of the freedmen before slavery was abolished, he said that " Mere discriminations on account of race or color were not regarded as badges of slavery." The first Mr. Justice Harlan dissented, in prophetic terms. He said: " If the constitutional Amendments be enforced, according to the intent with which, as I conceive, they were adopted, there cannot be, in this republic, any class of human beings in practical subjection to another class, with power in the latter to dole out to the former just such privileges as they may choose to grant. The supreme law of the land has decreed that no authority shall be exercised in this country upon the basis of discrimination, in respect of civil rights, against freemen and citizens because of their race, color, or previous condition of servitude." [9]

This decision has stood for more than eighty years.

[9] 109 U.S. at 25, 62.

Historically, it forms part of the "Compromise of 1877," which grew out of the close Presidential election of 1876. In that election, Samuel J. Tilden of New York, a Democrat, won a majority of the popular vote, but a number of decisive electoral votes were disputed. The controversy was put before a specially constituted Electoral Commission, which, at the last minute, decided in favor of Rutherford B. Hayes of Ohio, a Republican. We now know that this decision was the result of political arrangements, through which the North ceased its efforts at "reconstruction" in the South and the South was in effect left free to handle matters in its own way.[10] While this political settlement had no direct bearing on the questions of constitutional law which came before the Supreme Court, the atmosphere of the time was greatly affected by it. Indeed for the next fifty years there was only deterioration in the field of racial discrimination.

Many of the discriminations which have persisted in America, particularly in the Southern States, found their support in the Supreme Court's decision in the *Civil Rights Cases*. In recent times, however, the decision has been qualified in various ways. For example, Congress has been held to have power, through the Commerce Clause, to require the elimination of discrimination in interstate transportation.[11] There cannot be discrimination in premises which are publicly owned,[12] and this rule has recently been extended to a privately operated restaurant in a State-owned parking garage.[13] Lately the courts have found "State action"

---

[10] For a detailed discussion see Woodward, *Reunion and Reaction—The Compromise of 1877 and the End of Reconstruction* (1951).

[11] *Mitchell* v. *United States*, 313 U.S. 80 (1941).

[12] *Holmes* v. *City of Atlanta*, 350 U.S. 879 (1955) (*per curiam*).

[13] *Burton* v. *Wilmington Parking Authority*, 365 U.S. 715 (1961).

behind ostensibly private discrimination in a number of so-called " sit-in " cases,[14] and cases now pending may bring further developments in this area. Questions of this sort are also involved in the Civil Rights Act of 1964, recently passed by Congress, in which Congress has expressly relied on its power under the Fourteenth Amendment, and also on its power under the Commerce Clause. Nevertheless, whenever you read about a " sit-in " case, you can think of the decision of the Supreme Court in 1883 in the *Civil Rights Cases*, which has, until 1964, left self-help as the only remedy for the Negro in many parts of the country.

In two other nineteenth century decisions, the Court provided us with a reading of the " equal protection " clause of the Fourteenth Amendment that has spawned much of the inequality existing to the present day.

The first of these is *Pace* v. *Alabama*,[15] decided in 1883, a few weeks before the decision in the *Civil Rights Cases*. The defendant in that case, a Negro man, had been convicted under a statute of Alabama which imposed a penalty of from two to seven years' penal servitude on " any white person and any negro " who " intermarry or live in adultery or fornication with each other." Cases of adultery or fornication between persons of the same race were subject to a fine of $100, or imprisonment for not more than six months. The contention was made on behalf of Pace that the discrimination in punishment violated the Fourteenth Amendment. But the Court, speaking through Mr. Justice Field, said: " There is in neither section any discrimination against either

---

[14] *Garner* v. *Louisiana*, 368 U.S. 157 (1961); *Peterson* v. *City of Greenville*, 373 U.S. 244 (1963); *Lombard* v. *Louisiana*, 373 U.S. 267 (1963).
[15] 106 U.S. 583 (1883).

race. . . . Section 4189 applies the same punishment to both offenders, the white and the black. . . . The punishment of each offending person, whether white or black, is the same."

The Supreme Court of the United States has recently agreed to review a decision involving the statute of Florida which forbids mixed marriages, between persons of different races.[16] Whether *Pace* v. *Alabama* will survive this decision will no doubt be learned in the fairly near future. But the *Pace* case is significant here because of the light it throws on the approach taken by the Supreme Court to problems in this area within twenty years after the close of the Civil War. I need not enlarge on the influence which this approach had on the development of civil rights in the United States over the past eighty years, and of the role which such decisions have played as the background of our present problems.

Finally I want to refer to one more nineteenth century decision. This is *Plessy* v. *Ferguson*,[17] decided in 1896. This case involved a statute of Louisiana, passed in 1890, which required railroads carrying passengers in the State to " provide equal but separate accommodations for the white, and colored races, by providing two or more passenger coaches for each passenger train, or by dividing the passenger coaches by a partition so as to secure separate accommodations : . . . No person or persons shall be admitted to occupy seats in coaches, other than, the ones, assigned, to them on account of the race they belong to." From this point of view it is hard to think of a clearer example of a violation of the Fourteenth Amendment's prohibition against State action

---

[16] *McLaughlin* v. *Florida*, probable jurisdiction noted April 27, 1964, 84 Sup.Ct. 1178.

[17] 163 U.S. 537 (1896).

denying to any person the equal protection of the laws. But the Supreme Court, in an opinion by Mr. Justice Brown, upheld the validity of the Louisiana statute. He said:

> "A statute which implies merely a legal distinction between the white and colored races—a distinction which is founded in the color of the two races, and which must always exist so long as white men are distinguished from the other race by color—has no tendency to destroy the legal equality of the two races, or reestablish a state of involuntary servitude. . . .
>
> We consider the underlying fallacy of the plaintiff's argument to consist in the assumption that the enforced separation of the two races stamps the colored race with a badge of inferiority. If this be so, it is not by reason of anything found in the act, but solely because the colored race chooses to put that construction upon it. . . . If the civil and political rights of both races be equal one cannot be inferior to the other civilly or politically. If one race be inferior to the other socially, the Constitution of the United States cannot put them upon the same plane." [18]

Mr. Justice Harlan again registered the lone dissent. Referring to the Thirteenth, Fourteenth and Fifteenth Amendments to the Constitution, he said:

> "These notable additions to the fundamental law were welcomed by the friends of liberty throughout the world. They removed the race line from our governmental systems."

And he said:

> "The white race deems itself to be the dominant race in this country. And so it is, in prestige, in achievements, in education, in wealth and in power. . . . But in view of the Constitution, in the eye of the law, there is in this country no superior, dominant, ruling class of citizens. There is no caste

[18] *Id.* at 543, 551–552.

here. Our Constitution is color-blind, and neither knows nor tolerates classes among citizens. In respect of civil rights, all citizens are equal before the law. The humblest is the peer of the most powerful. . . .

The destinies of the two races, in this country, are indissolubly linked together, and the interests of both require that the common government of all shall not permit the seeds of race hate to be planted under the sanction of law. What can more certainly arouse race hate, what more certainly create and perpetuate a feeling of distrust between these races, than state enactments, which, in fact, proceed on the ground that colored citizens are so inferior and degraded that they cannot be allowed to sit in public coaches occupied by white citizens? That, as all will admit, is the real meaning of such legislation as was enacted in Louisiana." [19]

Few more prophetic statements can be found in the law books. Thus was fastened upon us, for nearly fifty years, the doctrine of " separate but equal." This decision gave the legal foundation for segregated schools, which were widely adopted not only in the South but in many other parts of the country. Nothing could more firmly have fastened prejudice into the hearts and minds of so many of our people. Separated from each other in school, the white child grew up conscious of his superiority, and of the degraded state of the Negro; and the Negro child grew up with his inferiority drilled into him through the only public school he was allowed to attend. Of course, as might be expected, the " equal " in " separate but equal " was largely forgotten. Many Southern States spent only a small fraction of the amount per child in their Negro schools as they did in their schools for white children. And the salaries of Negro teachers were generally far below those of white teachers.

[19] *Id*. at 555, 559, 560.

With a few exceptions, the physical plants available for Negro children were far inferior to those provided for white children. " Separate but equal " on trains and buses, and in schools, meant, in practice, racial discrimination of the clearest sort.

Thus we struggled along for forty years. This was the period when I was a boy, when I was studying the history of the United States—the Declaration of Independence, with its affirmation that " all men are created equal," the Civil War, with the freeing of the slaves, and the adoption of the great provisions of the Thirteenth, Fourteenth and Fifteenth Amendments. I lived in the North, and attended a non-segregated school. But I could see signs of discrimination all around me; and I learned about such things as the *Civil Rights Cases*, and *Plessy* v. *Ferguson*, and I was puzzled. Ours is a great country, with great traditions. We have claimed to be the home of liberty, and we went through a Revolution from the Mother Country to provide that liberty, and through the fire of a Civil War to preserve and extend that liberty. And what had we done with it? These were puzzling questions to me as a student. They did not become any clearer to me as a young lawyer.

Recent Forward Steps

But in the course of time there began to be a change in the tide. I cannot begin to go through all the details. From the beginning, the Supreme Court had held that there could not be discrimination on the ground of race with respect to jury service.[20] Though this is hard to enforce as a practical

---

[20] *Ex parte Virginia*, 100 U.S. 339 (1880); *Strauder* v. *West Virginia*, 100 U.S. 303 (1880).

matter, because of such things as peremptory challenges, which can be provided in sufficient numbers to enable the prosecutor to strike all or most Negroes from the jury, it has been an important matter, partly because it was long the only civil right which was directly enforced by the Court in favor of Negroes.

In the 1930's the Supreme Court decided the Scottsboro cases, which for the first time assured the right to counsel in capital criminal cases.[21]   The defendants in those cases were Negroes, and the decision was of great importance in helping to provide equality before the law for Negroes charged with crime.   And there were important cases involving voting rights, particularly with respect to the so-called " white primary " in the South.[22]   The Supreme Court held in 1917 that a municipal zoning ordinance which undertook to segregate the housing of a city was invalid.[23]   And a most important development in this area came in 1948, when the Court held that restrictive covenants against sale to Negroes or occupancy by Negroes in private deeds and contracts could not be enforced.[24]   Clearly the walls were crumbling.   And as cracks appeared, the pressures mounted.   They will surely continue until all legal bases of discrimination have been eliminated.

In the 1930's, too, cracks began to appear in the decisions as to education.   In this process, the situation as to legal education played a considerable part.   The first case was

[21] *Powell* v. *Alabama*, 287 U.S. 45 (1932).

[22] *Nixon* v. *Herndon*, 273 U.S. 536 (1927); *Nixon* v. *Condon*, 286 U.S. 73 (1932); *Smith* v. *Allwright*, 321 U.S. 649 (1944), overruling *Grovey* v. *Townsend*, 295 U.S. 45 (1935).

[23] *Buchanan* v. *Warley*, 245 U.S. 60 (1917).

[24] *Shelley* v. *Kraemer*, 334 U.S. 1 (1948).

Missouri ex rel. Gaines v. *Canada*,[25] which involved a Negro resident of Missouri who wanted to go to law school. Missouri had a law school at its state university, but at that time Negroes were not allowed admission there. So Missouri said that it would pay Gaines' expenses at a law school outside of Missouri which would take him. The Supreme Court held that where the State operated a law school for white students within the State, provision for legal education for Negroes outside the State was not equality. Then, in 1950, came the case of *Sweatt* v. *Painter*.[26] This involved a Negro law student in Texas. That State had a fine law school at its State University, to which only white students were admitted. Sweatt applied for admission, and was refused. At about this time, the State opened a new law school for Negroes, at the Texas State University for Negroes. The Texas courts found that the new school provided equal facilities for law study. But the Supreme Court, in an opinion by Chief Justice Vinson, refused to accept this conclusion. It compared the facilities and the reputations of the two schools and found them to be far from equal. It concluded that " the Equal Protection Clause of the Fourteenth Amendment requires that petitioner be admitted to the University of Texas Law School." On the same day, the Court held that the University of Oklahoma could not require a Negro student attending classes with white students to occupy separately designated seats in the classroom, in the library and in the cafeteria.[27]

---

25 305 U.S. 337 (1938).
26 339 U.S. 629 (1950). See also *Sipuel* v. *Board of Regents*, 332 U.S. 631 (1948).
27 *McLaurin* v. *Oklahoma State Regents*, 339 U.S. 637 (1950).

It pointed out that these restrictions impaired the Negro's opportunities for discussions with other students; and it concluded:

> ". . . that the conditions under which this appellant is required to receive his education deprive him of his personal and present right to the equal protection of the laws. . . . Appellant, having been admitted to a state-supported graduate school, must receive the same treatment at the hands of the state as students of other races."

Anyone who cared to look could see that *Plessy* v. *Ferguson* was becoming an anachronism, not only a social anachronism, but also a constitutional and legal anachronism. It could not really have been a surprise, therefore, when the Supreme Court held that the doctrine developed in these more recent cases applied to education generally, and that segregation in public education was a denial of the equal protection of the laws. Thus " separate but equal " was ended, as a legal and constitutional doctrine, and *Plessy* v. *Ferguson* was in effect, though not expressly, overruled. This was in the case of *Brown* v. *Board of Education*,[28] in a unanimous opinion written by Chief Justice Warren.

Nothing, I suppose, could more clearly show the ebb and flow of doctrine in constitutional litigation in the United States. And this development shows, too, the necessity, in our system, for the opportunity to make a fresh assessment of great constitutional questions from time to time. It is true that *Plessy* v. *Ferguson* had been decided, and was a basis for the rule of stare decisis. But more and more people came to think it was wrongly decided, and that it was in fact a very serious defect in our constitutional system. This was not a matter which could be corrected by Act of Congress.

[28] 347 U.S. 483 (1954).

Unless it was reconsidered by the Court, it could only be changed by a constitutional amendment. This is a very difficult and time-consuming process, requiring, by one method of procedure, a two-thirds vote in both Houses of Congress, and ratification by the legislatures or by conventions in three-fourths of the States. That might have been attempted. Yet, the mistake, if it was one, was the Court's mistake. The Court was in the best position to evaluate the situation and to conclude what it should do in the light of all the circumstances. Of course, one of the important circumstances was the earlier decision, which would be given great weight and respect. The Court does not lightly overrule one of its earlier decisions. But when the time comes, when it becomes apparent that the earlier decision on a constitutional question was wrong, and that it is a serious barrier to proper development and progress, our Court has always felt free to overrule the earlier decision and to declare the law as it thinks it should be. This power is, I think, essential to the sound development and operation of a constitutional system.

CIVIL RIGHTS TODAY

The *Brown* case is, naturally enough, a dividing point in the field of civil rights. Everything before the *Brown* decision is now background and history. Things since the *Brown* decision are current events, with many ramifications now before us.

It is sadly apparent that there are many Americans who do not really share the American ideal of liberty and equality for all citizens. We proudly recite the Declaration of Independence; we sing about " Sweet land of liberty," or " The land of the free and the home of the brave." But there are still many of our citizens who do not really believe these things deep down in their hearts. Many of these disbelievers live in the South, but there are many in other parts of the country, too. These citizens are the victims of prejudice which it will take us a long time to cure. To some extent, these prejudices continue to exist because of the doctrines of " separate but equal," and the related rule of the *Civil Rights Cases* which the Supreme Court fastened on us sixty-eight and eighty-one years ago. The task of ameliorating these prejudices is a great and arduous one. We are working on it—earnestly and diligently. We will not succeed all at once, but we will, I am sure, succeed in the end.

In the time that remains, I shall try to indicate how far we have advanced already. Of necessity, I can do no more than summarize, because the total picture is complex. Perhaps it will help to examine separately the developments in each of the five categories into which the civil rights problems are typically classified: (1) Voting, (2) Education, (3) Employment, (4) Housing, and (5) Administration of Justice.

Before going further, however, I would like to say a word of caution. Some of the situations in the United States are deplorable, to put it mildly. But when one goes through a listing of such situations, the net impression may be misleading. All of the circumstances which I will list are true. But the United States is a vast country, and many other things are true, too. There are many good things about relations between the races in the United States, and many individuals, of both races, have done much to contribute to these relations. Race relations in the United States, bad as they are in some ways, could be much worse. And, despite the tensions, in many ways they are better now than they were a generation ago, or ten years ago.

The very fact of increased pressure by Negroes to have their rights fully recognized is clear evidence of the improved position of Negroes in our community, and of their increased initiative in their own interests. We may be approaching a new recognition of the equal rights before the law of all men, regardless of race. When we have fully achieved that goal, the United States will have gone far to fulfill its destiny. If we cannot achieve such a state of true legal equality, the United States will no longer deserve a place of leadership among nations. This is truly our testing ground. Many of us hope and believe that we will meet the test, despite the fact that a depressing number of our countrymen do not truly believe in the things our country, through its history and potential destiny, really stands for.

Voting

Let us turn, first, to the position of the Negroes in the United States with respect to voting. We have seen the provision of the Fifteenth Amendment which purports to say that the right to vote shall not be denied on account of race. In large parts of the country, particularly in the North, this provision is followed to the letter. But, though the legal situation is the same, the practical situation with respect to voting in many of the Southern States is very different.

I cannot recount the whole story, but I believe two examples will suffice to show the devices which have been used to deprive Negroes of their constitutional right to vote. First, let us take the case of the town of Tuskegee, in Alabama. This is the site of Tuskegee Institute, an educational institution of high standing which was established in the last century exclusively for Negroes. Until 1957, Tuskegee was a square-shaped city, with about 400 Negro voters, many of them teachers or employees at the Institute, some with advanced University degrees. But by a statute passed by the Alabama legislature in 1957, Tuskegee became an irregular, twenty-eight sided city, from which all but 4 or 5 Negro voters (but no white voters) had been excluded. Eventually the validity of this arrangement came before the Supreme Court, where it was held invalid.[29] Most of the Court rested this conclusion on the Fifteenth Amendment, holding that the State legislation deprived the Negro voters of the right to vote on the ground of race. Mr. Justice Whittaker rested the same conclusion on the Fourteenth Amendment, on the ground that Negro citizens had been " fenced out of " Tuskegee, and thus had been segregated by State action.

Most other attempts to disfranchise the Negroes have been much more subtle than that in Tuskegee. An illustration may be found in Louisiana, where the Civil Rights Commission of the United States held hearings in 1960 and 1961. From the beginning, the State authorities in Louisiana refused to allow the Commission to inspect registration and voting records. The Commission's staff prepared a set of interrogatories for the voting registrars, and submitted this to the State attorney general, who advised the registrars not to answer the questions. When the Commission then scheduled a hearing, in 1959, the State attorney general, acting as counsel for the registrars, filed a suit to enjoin the Commission. The local Federal district court granted an injunction,

---

[29] *Gomillion* v. *Lightfoot*, 364 U.S. 339 (1960). For a popular discussion, see Taper, *Gomillion versus Lightfoot—The Tuskegee Gerrymander Case* (1962).

but this was reversed on appeal to the Supreme Court.[30] Finally, in 1960, the first of the hearings was held.

These hearings and other investigations disclosed that by 1956 only 10·3% of voting age Negroes were registered in Louisiana. By 1962, a concerted campaign in which the State was heavily implicated reduced this small percentage still further to 6·9%.[31] A variety of devices were used. For example, registration rolls were purged. Negroes could not find the registrars, though white persons had no difficulty. All persons seeking to register had to be identified by two registered voters. In districts where no Negroes were registered, it was impossible for Negroes seeking to register to obtain such identification, since white voters would not identify them. When these hurdles were passed, registrars would reject applications because they said there were " mistakes " in them. In one case, it appeared that the " mistake " was that the applicant had underlined the word " Mr." on the card instead of circling it. Then we come to a provision of the Constitution of Louisiana which says that voters must give their exact age, and this is construed to mean that the age must be given in years, months and days. Consider your own age in years, months and days, and how easy it would be to make an error in that computation. The registrars often found errors when the applicant was a Negro. Often, the Negro applicants were not told in what way they had failed to meet requirements.

If these devices are not used, there is yet another. Louisiana law requires any applicant to give a reasonable interpretation of any clause of the Louisiana Constitution, or

---

[30] *Hannah* v. *Larche*, 363 U.S. 420 (1960).
[31] *Report of the U.S. Comm'n on Civil Rights* 33 (1963). See also *Report of U.S. Comm'n on Civil Rights : Voting*, vol. 1, 41, 42, 43 (1961).

of the Constitution of the United States. Sometimes these interpretations were required to be in writing. In one case, a white applicant who wrote " I agree " after the constitutional provision was allowed to register. It is not surprising that Negro applicants could not satisfy the registrar that they had given a satisfactory interpretation. In some parishes there was evidence of intimidation. In one parish, where Negroes did register to vote in considerable numbers, they were forced to use segregated voting machines. All of this has been reported by the Civil Rights Commission.[32]

Many other instances could be given, but these will give the flavor of the problem, and show the lengths to which State officials and State legislatures will go to evade their Constitutional responsibilities. Constant pressure is maintained to redress these wrongs, but it is a vast undertaking on which progress has so far been very slow.

Why is nothing done about it? How do you proceed against a massive determination to break the law? This puts one aspect of the civil rights problem in a nutshell. We had one Civil War over this general issue, and understandably do not want to have another. It is easy to say, as many have said to me in other countries: " Well, you say it is against the law. Why don't you enforce the law? " It is far harder to make the law truly effective. Many people are trying. The Department of Justice has started many suits under the Civil Rights Act of 1957, but because of interminable delays, they have so far resulted in the registration of only a relative handful of voters.[33] With slow changes in outlook and in

[32] Vol. 1, *id*. at 39–68; *Report of U.S. Comm'n on Civil Rights* 18–19 (1963).
[33] See *id*. at 13–26, 37–50.

political leadership, particularly in the South, we can eventually make some progress, and I hope we will do so. But it is going to be a long slow road.

I want to emphasize that the problem must be kept in perspective. Of 50 States in the United States now, there appear to be only 8 in which there is serious discrimination against Negroes in voting. Of the 12 Southern States, there are 4 (Arkansas, Texas, Oklahoma and Virginia) where "Negroes now appear to encounter no significant racially motivated impediments to voting." [34] Restrictions on the right to vote are found in 8 States—Alabama, Florida, Georgia, Louisiana, Mississippi, North Carolina, South Carolina, and Tennessee. Less than 40% of the Negro population resides in these States. In three of these States, the Civil Rights Commission found that discrimination existed in only a few isolated counties. These are Florida, North Carolina, and Tennessee. And in the five other States, there is significant Negro registration. Discrimination exists there on what might be called a "local option" basis. [35] Altogether there are about 100 counties in the 8 Southern States where significant discrimination in voting exists. [36] It helps to reduce the problem to these more finite proportions. The Department of Justice now has suits pending in many of these 100 counties, and we may see progress in the days ahead. But we should not expect too much too soon.

Education

We have already referred to the case of *Brown* v. *Board of Education*, [37] which was decided on May 17, 1954, a little

[34] *Report of U.S. Comm'n on Civil Rights : Voting*, vol. 1, 22 (1961).
[35] *Ibid.*
[36] *Id.* at 23.
[37] 347 U.S. 483 (1954).

more than ten years ago. That was a great milestone in our constitutional history, and, of course, it did more than anything else to initiate a change of atmosphere in the United States, and to open the way for some of the pressures with which we are now confronted. But the sad fact is that today, ten years after that decision, very little or no progress has been made toward putting the decision into effect in six southern States. The situation may be graphically shown by giving the following figures which were reported in May, 1964: [38]

	School Districts with Negroes and Whites	Desegregated
Alabama	114	4
Florida	67	16
Georgia	181	4
Louisiana	67	2
Mississippi	150	0
South Carolina	108	1

In the South as a whole, there is some integration in 443 of the 2,256 school districts which have students of both races; and only 1·18% of all Negroes in Southern schools attend classes with white students.[39] Even in States where some progress has been made, as in Virginia, we have such situations as that in Prince Edward County, where all schools have been closed. White children have been educated in private schools for several years. Until a year ago, Negro children received no education at all, for more than three years. A year ago, due to the efforts of some public spirited citizens, mostly from other areas, some schools were opened

[38] Southern School News, May 1964, p. 1-A.
[39] *Ten Years in Review*, Southern School News, May 17, 1964, p. 1, cols. 3–5.

for them. Very recently the Supreme Court has held that Prince Edward County must reopen its State schools,[40] but the sad story is not yet completed.

During this period, we have had the Little Rock episode, and the sad events in Oxford, Mississippi, and in Alabama. In each of these instances, the force of the United States, represented by troops under the command of the President, was brought to bear against the intransigent opposition of the governors of these three States. These governors were defying decisions of the Courts, and asserting their views of " States' Rights," quite as if the Civil War had never been fought, and the Thirteenth, Fourteenth and Fifteenth Amendments to the Constitution had never been adopted. It has been observed that " the mayor or governor who invites resort to [violence] . . . resembles the camper who builds a roaring fire in a dry forest swept by a high wind. Maybe he can confine it to the job he wants it to do, but the odds are that he cannot." [41]

All of these governors had taken an oath to support and defend the Constitution of the United States, as well as of their own State. Yet they put their State views ahead of their obligations to the United States. I am told that in Alabama the Confederate flag flies over the State capitol in place of the flag of the United States. This is perhaps a graphic index of the problem with which we are confronted. It is a national tragedy of majestic proportions that the conclusion of this problem wrought by the Civil War has not been accepted by many of our citizens in the South; and it is

[40] *Griffin* v. *County School Board of Prince Edward County*, 377 U.S. 218 (1964).
[41] Lusky, " Racial Discrimination and the Federal Law: A Problem in Nullification," 63 *Colum.L.Rev.* 1163, 1174 (1963).

a tragedy, too, that political leadership in the South has seized on this, and sought to capitalize on it, without regard to the great moral problems involved.

But the problem is not confined to the South. Though there is no legal school segregation in the Northern States, and has not been for many years, there are in many parts of the United States, including the North, residential patterns such that certain areas are inhabited largely or exclusively by Negroes. As a result, schools in these areas are attended only by Negro children, or very largely by Negro children. Whether this " de facto " or " practical " segregation violates any provision of the Federal Constitution is not wholly clear. But there are many who believe that schools in northern cities should be " balanced," and that this should be achieved by moving students about, or " bussing " students from one area to another, as it is sometimes put. Just how this problem will work out is far from clear. Many of the parents whose children are " bussed," or whose children go to schools which were formerly all white, and are now expected to take in large numbers of Negro students, are as intransigently in opposition as any of their fellow citizens in the Southern States. So the problem is very much with us in the North.

In the *Brown* case, the Supreme Court decreed that action to end segregation in education should proceed " with all deliberate speed," [42] and commentators of the realist school have observed that " the system would have worked no differently in any event, no matter what the form of the Supreme Court's decree." [43] But " deliberate speed " has not been great speed. After ten years a good number of schools

---

[42] *Brown* v. *Board of Education*, 349 U.S. 294, 301 (1955).
[43] Bickel, " The Decade of School Desegregation: Progress and Prospects," 64 *Colum.L.Rev.* 193, 201 (1964).

have been integrated; yet often, after integration has taken place, white parents have moved away and the school has become limited to Negro students once more. This has happened in many of the schools in Washington, D.C. Many dedicated persons have wrestled with these problems for the past ten years, but the progress has been slow and disappointing. One of the factors in the picture, which we are just beginning to appreciate, is that Negro students, having long been deprived of adequate educational opportunities, now need extra effort and extra expenditures to bring them up to a level approaching equality. At long last, we may come to recognize more clearly our obligations in this area, and take the steps to meet them effectively.

Employment

Many people believe that the racial problem in the United States is essentially economic, and that when adequate employment opportunities are offered for Negroes, so that they can rise in the general economic scale, the other problems of discrimination will disappear. This is a great oversimplification, but there can be no doubt that the problem of employment is of great importance.

Until the Civil War, most Negroes in the United States were slaves, and most of them were doing the heavy labor on the cotton plantations of the South, or in related activity, such as teaming, shipping on the inland waterways, and so on. Most of them were not qualified for other types of work, and it is not surprising that they continued mostly as laborers after Emancipation. For fifty years, they remained chiefly in the South. But beginning with the First World War, more and more of them have moved to the industrial cities of the North, attracted by the employment opportunities there.

Generally speaking, though, the situation has been that they have been hired for the most menial work; and, in times of slack employment, they have tended to be the first employees who were laid off.

Until twenty years or so ago, this was the situation, and little was done about it. During the Second World War, when there was a shortage of available workers, there were the first few stirrings toward providing something approaching equal employment opportunities. On June 25, 1941, President Roosevelt issued Executive Order No. 8802, which established a five-man Fair Employment Practices Committee, responsible only to the President. As the Civil Rights Commission has said, "This was in many respects a landmark." [44] As the Fair Employment Practices Committee said in its Final Report, perhaps too optimistically, "The conscience of the nation was aroused." [45] But there was deep Southern opposition, and the Committee never received support from Congress. "F.E.P.C." became a label of opprobrium, and in 1946, as a result of Congressional action, the Committee was terminated. As an index of the situation, it may be observed that at the commencement of the Second World War, there were no Negroes in the United States Navy except in menial places, such as mess boys. [46] Negroes fought in the United States Army, but in segregated units.

At the close of the war, we were about where we had started, except for the conscience pricks which had come from the Fair Employment Practices Committee. In 1948, President Truman, as Commander in Chief of the Army and

---

[44] *Report of U.S. Comm'n on Civil Rights: Employment*, vol. 3, 10 (1961).
[45] P. 3 (1946). See also Norgren & Hill, *Toward Fair Employment* 149–79 (1964).
[46] U.S. Comm'n on Civil Rights, *Freedom to the Free* 114–15 (1963).

Navy, ordered the end of segregation in the Armed Services. But it was not until 1955 that the Department of Defense announced that the integration of all units of the regular armed forces had been accomplished. Even today, this has not been done with all reserve units and with all elements of the National Guard, which, in peace time, are primarily under State command and control.

The Government also provides much employment other than in the Armed Forces, and it is also the creator of employment through Government contracts and grants in aid. Here progress in recent years has been fairly good, though not complete. Both Presidents Kennedy and Johnson have done much to provide employment for Negroes in Government service, and old patterns are slowly breaking down.

With respect to private employment, we still have far to go. A number of States have Fair Employment Practices Commissions, and these have done much good. All of these, however, are in the North. They generally proceed by persuasion, and an employer who is determined to discriminate can usually find ways to do so, or to delay matters so long that the prospective Negro employee has been forced to find another job. A part of the problem lies in discrimination in training and in placement. It is hard for Negroes to find opportunities to be taken on as apprentices, which means that they cannot qualify for skilled employment. And in many States in the South, employment offices, even some which are financed with Federal funds, are operated on a wholly segregated basis. As a result, the Negro finds great difficulty in finding anything except unskilled employment. And it is hard for him to feel that it is worth while to take vocational training in school, because he knows that adequate employment opportunities will not be available for him even if he does get the requisite training.

Another source of discrimination is in labor unions. Many will not accept Negro members, which means that Negroes find great difficulty in obtaining employment as carpenters, metal workers, electricians, and so on, since contractors on substantial projects will hire only workmen who are members of the union. Sometimes this discrimination is justified on disingenuous grounds. At hearings held by the Civil Rights Commission in Newark, New Jersey, in 1962, union officers testified under oath that there was no discrimination in their unions. It was true, they said, that they had no Negro members, but this was because no Negro had ever applied. It was later pointed out that in these unions, no one could apply except on the endorsement of union members, and that, as a matter of practice, these unions did not take as members any persons who were not sons, or perhaps grandsons, of persons who were already members of the union. Thus, they had never refused membership to a Negro; but it was clear that, on this basis, they would never be forced to make a decision.

In 1961, President Kennedy by Executive Order [47] established the President's Committee on Equal Employment Opportunity, of which Lyndon B. Johnson, then Vice President, was Chairman. This committee, which was the successor of similar committees established by Presidents Truman and Eisenhower, deals primarily with discrimination in Federal Government employment and Federal Government contract employment. While achieving some success with

[47] Exec. Order No. 10925, 26 Fed. Reg. 1977 (1961).

Government contract employers through persuasion, the Committee's limited authority and resources make it relatively ineffective in the more difficult situations.

In a time of relative prosperity, such as we have had in recent years, efforts like these do have some impact, and it can be said that the employment picture has improved. More Negroes are finding better jobs. But large numbers of Negroes remain unskilled and find it hard to obtain employment. The picture can perhaps be best illustrated by breaking down a figure which is often used in discussing the problem of unemployment in the United States. This is the fact that unemployment now runs at the rate of about 5.4% of the working force. But Negro unemployment is about 10%; and unemployment among young Negroes, under twenty, looking for work, is about 20%. The latter figure is particularly ominous. The Negro youth knows that it will be extremely difficult for him to get a job, especially an interesting or attractive job. This makes it hard for him to see that it is worth while for him to remain in school. As a result, the school drop-out rate among Negroes is high; and juvenile delinquency problems of one sort or another are a result. Thus, the problem of employment among Negroes is a basic one, which we are very far from disposing of satisfactorily.[48]

Congressional action is needed to support fair employment opportunity. If we can have such action, and continue the progress we have already slowly made, we may develop a situation where the Negro citizen, young or old, can look for employment on a basis of reasonable equality with other citizens of our country.

[48] See Norgren & Hill, *Toward Fair Employment* (1964).

Housing

Outside of the South, probably the most pervading aspect of discrimination in the United States now is in housing. As the Civil Rights Commission has found: " Housing . . . seems to be the one commodity in the American market that is not freely available on equal terms to every one who can afford to pay." [49] Much of the housing market is closed to Negroes and members of some other minority groups. The result is a heavy concentration of non-whites, usually in the decaying centers of our cities. And this leads to a pyramiding of problems. Tax revenues go down. Slums become worse. Leadership moves to the suburbs, while the need for improvements in transportation, welfare and municipal services becomes more critical in the cities.

The national capital, Washington, held within the fixed boundaries of the District of Columbia, has become the first of our large cities to have a majority of Negro inhabitants. The 1960 census showed that 54.8% of Washington's residents were non-white. Over 98% of these were Negro. They live in 44.1% of the homes. During the previous decade non-whites were sold 2.2% of the new houses of metropolitan Washington. They were rented less than one-tenth of the area's new rental units. Non-whites occupy over one-half of the metropolitan area's deteriorating housing, and some two-thirds of its dilapidated housing.[50] The situation is similar in hundreds of other American cities, perhaps worse in the North and West than in the South.

Of course, this is not wholly a legal problem. And the

[49] *Report of U.S. Comm'n on Civil Rights* 534 (1959).
[50] U.S. Comm'n on Civil Rights, *Civil Rights U.S.A.—Housing in Washington, D.C.* 2–3 (1962).

way to resolve it is far from clear. I have already pointed out that the Supreme Court has held that municipal ordinances requiring segregation are unconstitutional, and that private restrictive covenants against sale to Negroes or occupancy by Negroes are unenforceable. Yet the fact of discrimination remains. Restrictive covenants, though not enforceable in court, may well be practically effective in excluding Negroes as possible purchasers of property. And there are other devices. For example, a person building a housing development may provide that no person buying a house in the development can sell it to a person who has not received the approval of a majority of all the owners of the development. This has all the earmarks of reasonableness; yet it may in fact be a wholly effective means of maintaining segregation in the development.

In recent years much effort has been devoted to this problem. The actions of real estate brokers and lending agencies in maintaining discriminatory practices have long been effective as segregating agencies. Many of the housing loans, however, are made with money provided by the Federal Government, or are guaranteed by the Federal Government. More and more the Federal Government has been using its power over loans to limit discrimination. This has culminated in the Executive Order issued by President Kennedy on November 20, 1962.[51] This order directed Federal agencies to act to prevent discrimination in the sale or rental of " residential property and related facilities " owned by the Federal Government, or aided or assisted by it after November 20, 1962.[52]

[51] Exec. Order No. 11063, 27 Fed. Reg. 11527 (1962).
[52] See *Report of U.S. Comm'n on Civil Rights* 99 (1963).

What will actually be accomplished by this order remains to be seen. Experience shows that there is a large gap between the formulation of policy on these matters at the top and its actual implementation in concrete cases by men who often have no interest in effectuating the policy. Nevertheless the Executive Order is of great importance, and will, in all probability, eventually, though slowly, have an appreciable effect on the housing situation.

In addition to Federal action, chiefly with respect to the policies of lending agencies, important steps have now been taken by a number of the States. There are now at least 19 States and more than 55 communities which have anti-discrimination housing laws.[53] But the coverage of these laws varies considerably. Often they apply only to multiple unit housing, and thus do not apply to single family residences. In 1964 there were 11 States and 14 communities which had enacted antidiscrimination housing laws applicable to nongovernmentally assisted housing. The 11 States were Alaska, California, Colorado, Connecticut, Massachusetts, Minnesota, New Hampshire, New Jersey, New York, Oregon and Pennsylvania. The local communities included New York City, Chicago, Philadelphia and Pittsburgh, Pennsylvania.[54] These laws, though often comprehensive, are sometimes cumbersome and difficult to enforce. We have had such a law in my State of Massachusetts for several years. There have been a few proceedings under it, but I do not

---

[53] *Report of U.S. Comm'n on Civil Rights* 98 (1963).
[54] Some of these are listed in *Report of U.S. Comm'n on Civil Rights: Housing*, vol. 4, 122 (1961). Others have been adopted since that Report was published.

think that it can be said that it has had any great impact on the problem of discrimination in Massachusetts.[55]

This much can be said. There is no legally enforceable discrimination in housing in the United States. There is a great deal of private discrimination. Some of this is illegal; and the pressures, such as they are, are against discrimination. But this may be the last area in which America's long standing pattern of discrimination against Negroes will be effectively changed.

Administration of Justice

The ideal of our country is stated in great letters carved into the portal of the Supreme Court Building in Washington: "EQUAL JUSTICE UNDER LAW." Statistically I think that we have made considerable progress towards that goal. But the exceptions are striking and depressing.

In April, 1959, a Negro, Mack Charles Parker, was arrested on a charge of raping a white woman in Poplarville, Mississippi, and was placed in the Pearl River County jail in Poplarville, pending trial. A short time previously, the United States Court of Appeals for the Fifth Circuit had set aside the conviction of another Negro, Robert Lee Goldsby, on the ground that Negroes had been illegally excluded from the Mississippi jury by which he was tried.[56] During the night of April 24, 1959, Parker was taken from the jail by a group of white men, who shot him twice and dropped his body into the Pearl River.[57]

---

[55] See Mass. Advisory Comm. to the U.S. Comm'n on Civil Rights, *Discrimination in Housing in the Boston Metropolitan Area* 98 (1963).

[56] *United States ex rel. Goldsby* v. *Harpole*, 263 F. 2d 71 (5th Cir. 1959), *cert. denied*, 361 U.S. 838, 850 (1960).

[57] *Report of U.S. Comm'n on Civil Rights: Justice*, vol. 5, 41 (1961).

The Federal Bureau of Investigation offered to cooperate in investigating the case. Its Director has testified that many of the members of the lynch mob were identified, and that admissions were secured from some of them.[58] Murder is a State offense in the United States, and we still proceed generally by indictment. When the Pearl River County grand jury met that fall, they refused to find an indictment. In January, 1960, the Federal Department of Justice presented the case to a Federal grand jury. This could not be for murder, since that is not a Federal offense. The presentation was with a view to an indictment under one or another of several Federal statutes which undertake to guarantee to citizens their civil rights as provided in the Constitution. But the Federal grand jury found no violation of Federal law, and returned no indictment.

Mack Charles Parker was the last person known to have been lynched in the United States. He was the 558th Negro lynched in Mississippi since 1883, the 3,441st in the United States. Eighty-five percent. of all lynchings have taken place in 17 Southern States.[59] It is a sorry tale.

In 1963, again in Mississippi, Medgar Evans was shot at night and killed by a sniper's bullet. He was the Mississippi head of the National Association for the Advancement of Colored People and had been active in various civil rights activities, including efforts to get Negroes registered as voters. In this case, a white suspect was arrested. He was indicted by a Mississippi grand jury and was twice tried for the crime

---

[58] Testimony of J. Edgar Hoover, Director, Federal Bureau of Investigation, in Departments of State and Justice, the Judiciary, and Related Agencies—Appropriations for 1961, Hearings Before the Subcommittee of the House Committee on Appropriations, 86th Cong., 2d Sess. 359 (1960).
[59] *Report of U.S. Comm'n on Civil Rights : Justice*, vol. 5, 42 (1961).

of murder. There can be no doubt that the prosecuting officers of Mississippi did their professional best to present the evidence and to obtain a conviction. But at both trials the jury disagreed. The high water mark was six votes for conviction at the first trial, according to newspaper accounts. This was regarded as a great triumph for the forces of right and justice. Thus is progress measured in this difficult area. And it may be great progress indeed, over a period of only four years.

Just as failure to prosecute or unsuccessful prosecution has been a problem, so too has been over-prosecution. In recent years, civil rights protests of many kinds have brought new tests to our administration of justice. These have included Freedom Rides, sit-ins, demonstrations, and other actions designed to vindicate rights claimed by Negroes, or claimed for them by participating white citizens. The reaction to these assertions of rights has often been massive police resistance, mass arrests, police dogs, and violence. White persons who have gone to Southern States to work against discrimination have found themselves charged with degrading offenses, and have sometimes found it desirable to leave the State before trial.

The statement is often made that " They came down here to break our laws, and they must take the consequences." But this statement often begs the question. For the Freedom Riders were seeking to use buses or trains or terminal facilities on an unsegregated basis, which they were clearly entitled to do under the United States Constitution. The provisions of State law to the contrary, though long enforced, were plainly invalid. The Freedom Riders were seeking only to vindicate their clear rights. Yet hundreds of them were arrested in Jackson, Mississippi, and held at high bail, often under difficult or unreasonable conditions. And many of the people involved in sit-ins were acting against State laws requiring segregation, which State laws were clearly invalid. We are, I think, slowly working out of this problem. But the obsession of many people in the South that "They are coming here to break our laws" is deep-seated, and very persuasive to those who are in its thrall.

I do not have time here to go through all the problems that are presented in the name of justice. The situation is made especially difficult in our system, since generally the administration of ordinary criminal justice is a matter for the States, in which the Federal Government has no standing to interfere, in the absence of a violation of some sort of Federal right. Thus, if a State, or its officers, really want to discriminate in the administration of criminal justice, it is very difficult for anyone to do anything about it.

This is not entirely a matter of criminal justice. The problem also arises in civil cases—especially efforts to secure the right to vote, to obtain desegregated education, to obtain the right to use a public library, or golf course, or swimming pool or beach. Here endless delay may be the chief product of the plaintiff's efforts. In some ways, the problem on the civil side can be epitomized by the troubles in Alabama of the National Association for the Advancement of Colored People. The NAACP is a national organization formed about fifty years ago for the purposes indicated by its name. It is a New York membership corporation, with branches or chapter in every State.

In 1956, the Attorney General of Alabama brought suit in the Alabama State court to oust the Association from the

State because of its alleged failure to comply with Alabama statutes requiring foreign corporations to register with the Alabama Secretary of State. On the day the complaint was filed, the Alabama court granted an *ex parte* restraining order barring the Association from conducting any business within the State. Before the case was heard on its merits, the Association was adjudged in contempt for failure to comply with a court order directing it to produce various records, including its membership lists.

This decision was, in due course, reversed by the United States Supreme Court.[60] When the case went back to the State court, that court changed the ground of its decision. This, too, was reversed on appeal to the United States Supreme Court.[61] But during all this time the NAACP could not obtain a hearing in the Alabama courts. After a year's delay, it started proceedings in the United States District Court. These were dismissed,[62] and the United States Court of Appeals affirmed the dismissal.[63] This case, too, went to the United States Supreme Court, which reversed the decision and held that the Federal District Court should give the NAACP a hearing unless the State courts did so by January 2, 1962.[64]

On December 29, 1961, the State court entered a final decree enjoining the Association from doing business in Alabama. After another year's delay, the decree was affirmed by the Alabama Supreme Court.[65] This State decision was based entirely on State procedural grounds—which you will

[60] *NAACP* v. *Alabama ex rel. Patterson*, 357 U.S. 449 (1958).
[61] *NAACP* v. *Alabama ex rel. Patterson*, 360 U.S. 240 (1959).
[62] *NAACP* v. *Gallion*, 190 F.Supp. 583 (M.D.Ala. 1960).
[63] *NAACP* v. *Gallion*, 290 F. 2d 337 (5th Cir. 1961).
[64] *NAACP* v. *Gallion*, 368 U.S. 16 (1961).
[65] *NAACP* v. *State*, 274 Ala. 544, 150 So. 2d 677 (1963).

not believe when I summarize them. The Supreme Court of Alabama referred to " a rule of long standing and frequent application that where unrelated assignments of error are argued together and one is without merit, the others will not be considered." The Alabama court held that at least one of the assignments of error contained in each of the five numbered subdivisions of the " Argument " section of the NAACP's printed brief was without merit, and that it would therefore not consider the merits of any of the other assignments. This was said to be a purely non-Federal ground of decision which it was not in the province of the United States Supreme Court to review.

But the United States Supreme Court did review this decision, and reversed it.[66] The Supreme Court also considered the merits of the case, and held, nearly eight years after the NAACP had been enjoined from operations in Alabama, that it was entitled to conduct its activities there. It remanded the case to the Alabama Supreme Court to enter an appropriate order, and lugubriously concluded : " Should we unhappily be mistaken in our belief that the Supreme Court of Alabama will promptly implement this disposition, leave is given the Association to apply to this Court for further appropriate relief." This proceeding speaks for itself and tells much about our unhappy problem and the sad role which some lawyers and judges have played in it. This was made clear in an editorial (leader) in the *New York Times* a few days later,[67] which said :

> " Anyone who wonders why those involved in racial litigation in the South so often look to the Supreme Court for relief have only to study the latter's decision the other day in

[66] *NAACP* v. *Alabama ex rel. Flowers*, 377 U.S. 288 (1964).
[67] *N.Y. Times*, June 6, 1964, p. 22.

the case of the National Association for the Advancement of Colored People v. Alabama. The history of this case shows nothing less than a cynical perversion of the legal process by state judges sworn to uphold law and the Constitution."

The *Times* added:

"The whole case is a sordid example of the shabby tactics practiced these days under the banner of 'state's rights.'"

The situation is a regrettable one, but even more regrettable is the fact that it is not confined to the State courts. Some of the judges of the Federal courts, too, find it possible to fail to grant prompt remedies to those who invoke the power of the courts. This happens in some United States district courts, where each judge is pretty much a power unto himself in conducting the business of his court, until he is reversed by the United States Court of Appeals; and the Court of Appeals often cannot act until the district judge has decided the case. There have, too, even been some instances of obstruction and delay in the United States Court of Appeals.

This matter was recently examined in great detail in a Note in the *Yale Law Journal* on "Judicial Performance in the Fifth Circuit." [68] The case of James Meredith, who sought to enter the University of Mississippi, may be taken as an example. Meredith's suit was filed in May, 1961, but it was not until October, 1962, that he actually registered in the University. In the interval, five terms at the University came and went. Much of this delay, according to Circuit Judge Wisdom was "attributable to continuances of doubtful propriety and to unreasonably long delays by the trial judge." [69] Even after the Court of Appeals had acted, and had ordered

[68] 73 *Yale L.J.* 90 (1963).
[69] *Meredith* v. *Fair*, 305 F. 2d 343, 351–52 (5th Cir. 1962).

the case remanded to the trial court for entry of judgment in favor of Meredith, " Circuit Judge Cameron four times stayed the remand directive. Three times his stay was vacated by his brethren; finally Mr. Justice Black invoked his power to set aside the fourth stay order and thus effectuate the remand." [70]

In such cases there is little remedy available to the parties or to the public authorities. Once a Federal judge has been duly appointed, he can be removed only by impeachment—or by the hand of God, as has happened in the case of Judge Cameron. But there is little prospect of impeachment in these cases. And thus a judge may delay and obstruct as much as he feels desirable with little thought of any consequences to himself. When this happens with elected State judges, one may feel a certain understanding of human nature. When it happens to Federal judges, appointed for life, and sworn to support and defend the Constitution of the United States, one can only be sad at the failure of our profession, in these instances. The *Yale Law Journal* Note concludes with these words:

> " If the assumption of 'good will effort' by the trial judge to comply with the spirit and letter of higher court directives breaks down, then, the traditional tools by which the judiciary secures its internal discipline may be unequal to the task. . . . The chief difficulty arises not from behavior of judges but from the appointment of men who in important areas will not observe the self-discipline upon which an appellate system is premised. The principal cure must be found in the appointment of judges who will disinterestedly comply with decisions of higher courts." [71]

[70] 73 *Yale L.J.* at 92.   [71] *Id.* at 133.

But, it may be added, the appointment of such judges is not so easy when they must be confirmed by the United States Senate, acting through a Judiciary Committee of which the senior Senator from Mississippi is Chairman. It is a challenge to the highest political skill of the President, which I believe he will generally be able to meet.

The array of facts and figures I have presented should be helpful in presenting the civil rights situation as it exists in the United States, but they should not be allowed to obscure the human essence of the problem.

This factor, and its essential pettiness, can be shown by telling you about a case which recently went all the way to the Supreme Court of the United States.

In a suit in a State court in Alabama, Mary Hamilton, a Negro woman, was a party and a witness. Pursuant to the South's caste system, under which no Negro is addressed as Mr., Mrs., or Miss, cross-examining counsel, despite the witness's request to be called Miss Hamilton, or Miss Mary Hamilton, insisted on addressing her as "Mary." As she declined to answer questions when so addressed, the court held her in contempt, and sentenced her to five days in jail and a fine of fifty dollars.

A writ of certiorari was obtained from the State Supreme Court, but not until she had served the jail sentence. The State Supreme Court solemnly affirmed the judgment of the trial court, saying that "the question was a valid one and the witness invoked no valid legal exemption to support her refusal to answer it." [72] But counsel for Miss Hamilton were diligent, and the case went on its way to the United States Supreme Court. That Court summarily reversed the State

[72] *Ex parte Hamilton*, 275 Ala. 574, 156 So. 2d 926 (1963).

court's decision.[73]   It is too bad—but revealing—that such a matter had to become a question of constitutional law; but it is now the law of the land that a State court cannot enforce an invidious discrimination in the address of a witness—as it was only recently held that a State court cannot enforce racial segregation in its court room.[74]

CONCLUSION

There is perhaps hope in the thought recently advanced by Professor Louis Lusky, when he wrote:[75]

> " Men must act out the roles they have accepted, and, at least for a while, comply with the demands of the institutional mechanisms that prescribe the patterns of their outward lives.   But they can no longer do it happily. . . .   They can no longer confidently teach their children to emulate their own attitudes.   And therein lies the seed of significant change."

Indeed we have seen a change in America in the ten years since the Supreme Court spoke in 1954, but the pace has been slow.   Not all the blame for this pace can be laid at the door of the extreme conservatives who continue to fight a last-ditch battle for " States' rights."   As much of the onus may be laid to those of moderate persuasion who fail to speak up or take action.[76]   It is all the more lamentable when

---

[73] *Hamilton* v. *Alabama*, 376 U.S. 650 (1964).

[74] *Johnson* v. *Virginia*, 373 U.S. 61 (1963).

[75] Lusky, '' The Stereotype: Hard Core of Racism,'' 13 *Buffalo L.Rev.* 450, 456 (1964).

[76] See McGill, Book Review, *N.Y. Times Magazine*, May 10, 1964, p. 3, reviewing Morgan, *A Time to Speak* (1964).   See also Stringfellow, *My People Are the Enemy—A Polemical Autobiography* (1964), written by a graduate of the Harvard Law School, who has spent five years practicing law in East Harlem, New York City.

such persons are in positions of national leadership and responsibility.[77]   But even active crusaders for civil rights recognize that, to some extent, delay and gradualism are inherent in the problem itself.[78]

Despite its slowness, progress has been made.   A summary of this progress since the *Brown* decision has recently been given by Anthony Lewis, writing in the *New York Times* :[79]

1. It may, more than anything else, have given the Negro hope.

2. It gave the Negro a courage and a will that few, or even he himself, had known he had.

3. The struggle to carry out the school decision encouraged Negroes to speak out for other rights.

4. Violent Southern resistance to the School decision awakened Northern white opinion to the meaning of racism.

5. The Federal Government was at last moved to action in race matters.

6. These years have demonstrated the extraordinary role of law as a shaper of opinion in the United States.   As Mr. Lewis has written: "One of the terrible tragedies was the solemn advice of Southern leaders, perhaps most significantly Senator Harry F. Byrd of Virginia, that the law could be resisted with impunity.   It has taken much time and even the spilling of blood to demonstrate the difference between criticizing a court decision and organizing physical resistance to it.   The cost has been the degrading of the entire political process in one section of the country."

7. But a companion lesson is that law is not enough. Despite its shortcomings, the United States is a moralistic as well as a legalistic country.   Using Mr. Lewis' words again, " The young followers of Dr. King, sitting quietly at lunch

---

[77] See generally, Anderson, *Eisenhower, Brownell, and the Congress—The Tangled Origins of the Civil Rights Bill of 1956–1957* (1964).

[78] Marshall and Carter, " The Meaning and Significance of the Supreme Court Decree," 24 *J.Negro Ed.* 397, 402–03 (1955).   The authors were counsel in the *Brown* case.

[79] *N.Y. Times Magazine*, May 10, 1964, pp. 9, 91–94.

counters as they were verbally and physically abused, brought a needed spiritual content to the movement for racial justice."

Indeed, it is clear by now that what we are dealing with here is a national neurosis, which can only be expected to yield with long and patient treatment. Though we have always detested the caste system of India, the fact is that since Emancipation we have clearly maintained a caste system in the United States. For many citizens of our country, the Negro is the untouchable, and these citizens act and react accordingly. This is not solely a Southern problem, by any means. But the neurosis is more pervasive, more deep-seated, more disabling, in the South, generally speaking, than in other parts of the country. This disability is, of course, one of the greatest handicaps of the country. It would be far better for all, not merely for the Negro, if we could exorcise it. As Professor Walter Gellhorn has recently written, "Demolishing the caste system is probably the most urgently needed and potentially the most satisfying activity beckoning to today's young Americans." [80] We are moving towards this goal, but we still have a long way to go. I hope we will redouble our efforts in this undertaking, for it is one which we must complete—to use the words of President Kennedy —"not merely for reasons of economic efficiency, world diplomacy, and domestic tranquility—but, above all, because it is right." [81]

[80] Gellhorn, " A Decade of Desegregation—Retrospect and Prospect," 9 *Utah L.Rev.* 3, 17 (1964).
[81] *Civil Rights and Job Opportunities—Message from the President*, 109 Cong. Rec. 10533, 10538–39 (daily ed. June 19, 1963).

Chapter 6

ENVOI

In these lectures, I have tried to show some aspects of the development of the common law in the United States. In using certain problems for examples, I could easily leave a misleading impression. I have not talked about torts or contracts or agency, or even of company law or bills of exchange, where our law would be found to have many similarities to yours, and to owe much to yours for its origin and development. On the contrary, I have deliberately sought out some areas where our law and experience are quite different from yours.

I have done this in part to try to explain to you our situation so that you might perhaps not think us quite so barbaric as we must sometimes seem to you to be. But I have also done this in order to show that even in these areas where our problems are so different, we owe much to the blessings of the common law. Even in these areas we use an essentially common law approach. With the tools and the terms of the common law, we proceed, usually on a case by case basis, in the common law tradition.

You are fortunate indeed that you do not have these problems. Perhaps by pointing them out I comply with the terms of Miss Hamlyn's trust which require me to show you the blessings which the inhabitants of the United Kingdom derive from their indigenous version of the common law.

Proceeding with this theme, I take the liberty of putting my conclusion in words used last year by Lord Devlin in speaking to the Law Council of Australia:[1]

> ".... In the long list of countries that were once ruled from Britain, ... I cannot, as I speak, think of one, not one, that has not kept the common law. Some ... went their way easily and in peace, others in bitterness and in strife, ... Although even those who went their way most easily, might have been thought to want to get rid of any sort of reminder of tutelage none of them did so. In independence they changed many things, but not the English way of doing justice according to law. And why? Because, being free men, and having a free choice, they being solicitous to preserve the freedom they have won, they let it remain with them as their greatest safeguard. That's the test. Of all that imperial Rome gave to the world, there's not now much left. Monuments cannot speak nor a classic literature in a language that is dead. What still speaks is the Roman law which for many centuries after the decline of Rome remained the law of civilization, and is still the basis of the law of Europe. Because England was on the fringe of Rome's dominions, because she preferred to go her own way, and her own way of doing justice, it has spread them all over the new world to countries which Rome never knew, and it may be that when London is a buried city, and Westminster is only a name, and there's a new and greater society in which freedom is secure, that in its foundations there will be embedded the common law."

[1] Opening Address at Thirteenth Legal Convention of the Law Council of Australia, 36 *Australian L.J.* 277, 282 (1963).

(31)